The Mantram Handbook �%

EKNATH EASWARAN

Born into an ancient matrilineal Hindu family in South India, Eknath Easwaran was raised by the loving hands of his mother and his mother's mother, whom he regards as his spiritual teacher. She taught him by her selfless example how to find complete spiritual fulfillment in the family context by putting the welfare of those around her first.

In later years, while meditating earnestly, Easwaran followed a successful career as writer and teacher and was chairman of the English department of a large Indian university when he came to the U.S. on the Fulbright exchange program. In 1960 he established the Blue Mountain Center of Meditation in Berkeley, and since that time he has dedicated himself completely to teaching meditation to those leading active lives in the midst of family and community.

Besides *The Mantram Handbook,* Eknath Easwaran has written *Gandhi the Man* and *The Bhagavad Gita for Daily Living* and published his translations in *The Katha Upanishad* and *Three Upanishads: Īsha, Māndūkya, & Shvetāshvatara.* He also writes the articles in the Center's quarterly, *The Little Lamp.*

Eknath Easwaran

Introduction by Richard B. Applegate

The Mantram Handbook

Formulas for Transformation

NILGIRI PRESS

© 1977 by the Blue Mountain Center of Meditation
All rights reserved
Printed in the United States of America
Designed, printed, and bound by Nilgiri Press
First printing October, 1977; reprinted July, 1978
ISBN 0–915132–10–9

The Blue Mountain Center of Meditation, founded
in Berkeley in 1960 by Eknath Easwaran, publishes
books on how to lead the spiritual life in the home
and the community. Please write for information to
Nilgiri Press, Box 477, Petaluma, California 94952.

Library of Congress Cataloging in Publication Data
will be found on the last leaf of this book.

Dedicated to my beloved mother
EKNATH AMMAL KUNCHI AMMAL

Contents ❦

What the Mantram
Can Do ✳

The mantram is a short, powerful spiritual formula
for the highest that we can conceive of—whether we
call it God, or the ultimate reality, or Nature with a
capital *N*. Whatever name we use, with the mantram
we are calling up what is best and deepest in ourselves.

People often think of the mantram as an exotic
import from India or Tibet, and the word may bring to
mind an image of somebody seated cross-legged on the
floor chanting. But the mantram need not be exotic.
It has appeared in every major spiritual tradition, West
and East, because it fills a deep, universal need in the
human heart.

In the first part of *The Mantram Handbook,* you
will find directions for selecting and using a mantram.
The mantram is most effective when repeated silently,
in the mind. You don't have to chant it aloud, and it
doesn't require any fixed times or place or special

equipment. During the course of your day, you can repeat the mantram in your mind at almost any time—when you are walking, or brushing your teeth, or standing in line at the post office. This is no mere mechanical repetition; it drives the mantram deep into your consciousness, where it can begin to effect a marvelous transformation. The advertiser uses this same principle to persuade us to buy all sorts of things we don't need, but with the mantram we are making the power of the word work for us instead of against us.

The mantrams you will find in this book are of proven power. They have worked in the lives of many men and women before you. You can choose one of them and feel confident that it is a mantram with roots, bequeathed to us by one of the great spiritual teachers of the world's major traditions. But you don't have to change your religion or subscribe to any dogma to benefit from the mantram—you simply have to be willing to try it.

The second part of the book shows how the mantram becomes a powerful tool for getting some control over your life: cultivating beneficial habits, transforming negative emotions like anxiety or hostility, or gaining a real sense of purpose. The secret is that the mantram enables us to direct our attention at will, from negative to positive channels. Because we are usually not able to keep our attention focused, we often let the mind wander off in unproductive and even harmful directions. The mantram gives the mind something positive to hold on to so that we can make wise and intentional choices.

Let me give a few examples of how helpful this can be.

In times of distress—if you're sitting in the dentist's chair, for example, and your stomach is slowly tying itself in knots—the mantram gives your mind something to focus on besides your discomfort. A friend of mine who had to have a cavity filled without the benefit of Novocaine impressed the dentist by her calm. He knew she had been using the mantram, and he asked if it deadened the pain. "Oh, no," she replied. "But it did keep me from jumping through the roof."

When you are tense or worried, the problem is that the same few anxious thoughts are going around and around in your mind. It's like listening to a broken record: your attention has become stuck, and all you hear is "trouble, trouble, trouble." The mantram can pick the needle up from the place where it's stuck and move it on.

The mantram is a powerful ally in overcoming depression. With its help, you can free your mind from brooding on yourself and your problems. Most important, it can prevent the oscillations of the mind that lead to depression, so that you don't even have to let depression get its foot in the door to begin with.

If you're trying to make some beneficial change in your life, such as losing weight or giving up smoking, the mantram can strengthen your will so that a cigarette or a piece of pie won't get the better of you.

The mantram can reduce the friction we experience in daily personal encounters, which all too often stems not so much from anything the other person has done as from our own moods. If we haven't slept well, or if things aren't going our way, we often take it out on the people around us. The mantram reminds us that we still have it in us to be kind and patient, even if we *have* had a hard day.

Finally, we can use the mantram to begin repairing broken relationships. All of us have deeper resources for this than we realize, and the mantram enables us to draw upon those resources to bear cheerfully with people we find irritating, to respond to what's best in others even when we have serious differences, to transform anger into compassion and ill will into love. Nowhere is this skill more precious than in the home, between man and woman or parent and child. I am always deeply touched when someone who has started using the mantram tells me that now he can discuss politics with his father without losing his temper, or that she has been able to move closer to her husband when they were barely on speaking terms a few months before.

In the last part of the book, I show how the mantram relates to a larger body of spiritual disciplines—not dogmas or beliefs, but proven techniques which we can all put into practice to make our lives rich, purposeful, and fulfilling. With these techniques we can harness the immense resources within us to unify our personality and make a lasting contribution to life, knowing every day that we are needed and cherished by those around us. Most difficult of all, we can gain our own self-respect. This is the real glory of the human being, that we can choose to remake ourselves completely.

As a teacher of meditation, I cannot hide my partiality for meditation as the most powerful of these tools for transformation. But the mantram complements meditation beautifully, and even those who are not prepared to meditate can derive great benefit from the mantram.

Over a long period of time, the mantram can bring about far-reaching changes in our state of mind, gradually elevating our consciousness. This appeals to many people, but there are many more who are looking for something they can use and benefit from right now.

Here the mantram is an absolutely practical tool which we can use to develop evenness of mind in all the ups and downs of daily life.

With *The Mantram Handbook* going into another printing, I would like to take this opportunity to say how gratifying the response to the book has been. A number of readers have written to tell me how much the mantram has come to mean to them. Each in its own way, practically all of their letters say that they came across this book at a crucial time in their lives: when they needed it, were open to it, and were able to put it into practice.

EKNATH EASWARAN

Introduction: The Power of the Word

by Richard B. Applegate

The mantram, the holy name, often conjures up images of something occult or impractical to people from the West, who sometimes have difficulty believing that a name can have any special power. My purpose in this introduction is to show that all of us believe that names and words have power. This is attested not only in myth and scripture but also in folktales and folk beliefs, as well as in customs which we observe daily. On some deep level, all human beings feel that names are intimately associated with the person or thing they designate, and that the word can evoke the reality it describes.

Language is a symbolic intermediary between the external world and man's private internal world. We use this symbolic system constantly, not only for communication between two people but also in our own minds to sort out, conceptualize, and store many kinds of information. This constant use of a symbolic system invests the symbols themselves with power over the user. As a result, on some almost subconscious level we feel an intimate connection between name and thing, between word and deed. Consequently, the word and the name partake of the character of the thing; and conversely, the utterance of the name or the word has the power to evoke the thing named. This deep-seated awe of the word leads to a host of beliefs, superstitions, customs, and taboos, from which we in the twentieth century are hardly exempt.

The power of the word impresses itself upon us every time we speak or write, even in as simple a matter as our choice of vocabulary. In all languages, written or unwritten, we find a basic division of vocabulary into two or three levels—high and low, or (as in English) high, neutral, and low. For a great many concepts we must make a choice among a set of words which stand for the same thing, but which differ vastly in connotation. It is one thing to *die,* another to *expire,* and something else again to *croak.* We are very sensitive to these differences, and a word can be humorous or shocking when used in the wrong context. Here, we are reacting as much to the word itself as to what it stands for. *Die* is neutral; it has the fewest emotional overtones, and we can use it in the widest range of contexts. *Expire* is high vocabulary, which shows a certain dignity or stiffness. On this level we find technical, euphemistic, poetic or archaic expressions like *pass away* and *perish*. *Croak* is low vocabulary, in the sense that we do not accord words on this level the same dignity as high and neutral expressions. Words on the low level are largely restricted to childish, slangy, flippant, or vulgar usage.

These differences explain the humor and the shock value when words are used in inappropriate contexts, as in "My African violet expired from lack of water," or "His Royal Highness, the King of Eritrea, kicked the bucket last year." Innumerable other examples suggest themselves, such as *dine, eat,* and *shovel it down; countenance, face,* and *kisser;* or *progeny, children,* and *kids.* The differences among these expressions are only semantic, you may say, but at every turn we are forced to make such choices as we express ourselves. Our choice can keep others at a distance or draw them in; it can leave them untouched or move them to laughter or tears or anger.

In all cultures, ritual and religion tend to find expression in high vocabulary, using verbal symbols which evoke an aura of reverence, solemnity, and power. Thus in the King James Bible we find *brethren* for our everyday term *brothers, spake* for *spoke, thou* and *thy* for *you* and *your,* and so on. There are two main reasons for this association of religion with the high level of usage, and they work together. First, the dignity of this elevated level naturally makes it most appropriate for expressing matters of the spirit—and not only for matters of the spirit, in ritual and religion, but also for myth, much poetry, and very formal or solemn speech. The Gettysburg Address is a moving example of formal oratory in elevated language. Second, the language of ritual and religion is very often preserved intact while people's everyday speech gradually changes with the passage of time, so that religious language retains many archaic features. In King James's day, everyone said *brethren* as the plural of *brother,* but now *brethren* is distinctly archaic; its connotations are solemn, poetic, and scriptural. So the verbal symbols of religion evoke in us a sense of reverence, a connotation of some legacy from the past.

A great deal of meaning can be condensed into a single word, which evokes a powerful image pervading a tradition. The Zuñi Indians, like the ancient Hebrews, symbolize the spirit as breath or as wind. References to breath and wind occur frequently in Zuñi prayers, sacred chants, and religious oratory; an allusion to breath or wind can give religious overtones to an otherwise neutral utterance. In Christianity, the image of Christ as the shepherd and mankind as the sheep is central. Any reference to shepherd or pastor, to flock or lamb or lost sheep, can play upon this central image. Sometimes we forget that these images are culturally bound rather than universal. When European missionaries used pastoral images in China, it didn't work. As an agricultural people whose traditional antagonists had been the nomadic herding peoples to the north, the Chinese responded negatively to the image of the sheep and the Good Shepherd. The image which moved them was that of climbing the sacred mountain, an allegory of spiritual evolution used beautifully, for example, by the mystical poet Han Shan.

Often, we do not realize how deep our response to the verbal symbols of ritual and religion is until these symbols are tampered with. In 1903, a translation of the Bible from the traditional New Testament Greek into the vernacular of the people sparked rioting in Greece, so strongly did the Greek people feel that the archaic and elevated vocabulary of the original was the only fitting vehicle for scripture. A great many people today, including nonbelievers, feel that something has been lost in modern English renderings of the King James Bible. These modern renderings are clearer, but they often strike us as flat and pedestrian. When "Cast not thy pearls before swine" becomes "Don't throw your pearls in front of pigs," we feel that something tangible is missing. And many Catholics say that they preferred hearing the mass in Latin rather than in English, even if they understood only a little of the Latin, because the traditional language seemed richer and more holy. In all these cases, we find that part of our response is to the word itself, with its solemnity, its wealth of religious overtones, and its power.

In a larger sense, however, it is not only in the realm of religion, where feelings run high, but in every sphere of human activity that the power of the word evokes deep responses and strong reactions. Personal names are another area in which our deep awe of the word impinges on daily life. Many peoples believe that the name is an integral part of the person; the Eskimos, for example, say that body and soul and name together make up the whole person. In our own culture, we feel that our personal name is somehow linked with our identity. We often have a mental image of what sort of person ought to go with a particular name; all of us probably know people whose names suit them perfectly, or whose names don't suit them at all. Charles Dickens had such a masterful touch at matching names and characters that some of his invented names, like Scrooge, have passed into everyday parlance.

The association of name and person is evident in other ways too. Small children sometimes have difficulty understanding how more than one person can be called by the same name, and in some tribal societies, custom forbids that any two living members of the tribe should bear the same name. It is as if name and life-force are so intimately linked that sharing a name is dangerous because it attenuates the life-force of both parties. In

Egypt, children do not receive the names of living parents or grandparents. This is considered bad luck; one of the two would soon die.

Custom may permit a child to receive the name of a deceased relative; the Jews regard this naming practice as a memorial to the dead, a way of keeping the name of the dead alive. In some tribal societies of Africa and the New World, ancestral spirits are invited to rejoin the living by solemnly bestowing their names on newborn infants. Elsewhere it is assumed that the newborn are reincarnated ancestors, whose names are revealed in dreams or by divination to be bestowed on the child.

Naming practices reflect our belief that name and identity are linked. In the examples above, the ancestor's identity determines the child's name. In many cultures, names are not chosen; they are supernaturally predetermined. The Ojibwa, for example, expect a newborn child's name to be revealed to the mother or father in a dream. There is no choice in this, even though the Ojibwa feel that some names are lucky, making for success in life, while others are less auspicious. Another common naming practice is to name a child after some respected figure, someone powerful or long-lived, or someone who embodies a prized virtue. We find this custom in our own culture, where it is motivated not only by a desire to honor the namesake, but also by the hope that the child will take after the person for whom it is named.

So we see two recurrent themes in naming practices, both of which show the link between name and identity. The name can be a bond between the individual and his kin, a link between generations; in some societies, names can be owned by families or clans, in the sense that particular names are bestowed only within the clan. The name can also be an expression of the bearer's character, and names are even believed to have an influence on a person's good or bad fortune.

The monastic tradition of taking a new name upon entering a religious order also illustrates the link between name and identity. Both in Eastern and Western monasticism, men and women entering orthodox religious orders drop their old identity as they dedicate their lives to the quest for God. Just as adopting the habit or the cowl or the ochre robe symbolizes a new identity, so does assuming a new name like Sister Teresa or Brother Atulananda. The secular twentieth-century parallel is the adoption of stage names by actors and entertainers. Before they stepped into the limelight, many of these personalities had everyday names which could be those of somebody we went to school with or somebody who lives around the corner. But along with a glamorous public image goes a glamorous name to adorn the marquee. Boris Karloff, for example, would not seem half so sinister had he stayed William Henry Pratt.

This feeling that our name is an integral part of us gives rise to a host of beliefs, customs, and taboos. The strongest of these beliefs is that knowing a person's name gives the knower some power over that person, and consequently in cultures all over the world we find a reluctance to divulge or mention personal names. The motivation is often magical. Since in folk belief the name is an integral part of the person, it can be used for magical purposes, just as sorcery is said to make use of hair cuttings or nail parings or anything that has been in physical contact with a person. The belief is extremely widespread, and it gives rise to the very common custom of giving everyone two names. This was the practice of the ancient Egyptians and many other peoples of the ancient world, as well as of most tribal peoples in our own era. The real name is known only to parents and perhaps godparents, to husband or wife, and to a few trusted friends, while the lesser name, the name that is publicly known, is ineffective for magical purposes.

A milder version of this name taboo is the custom of not divulging anyone's name to a stranger, who is a potential enemy. There may be certain specific contexts in which using names is taboo, such as at night, when spirits might hear the name and call the person off to join them, or in potentially dangerous situations such as warfare, hunting, or even rituals. There may also be a taboo on a person saying his own name, even if others are permitted to. Name and breath are often thought to be an integral part of the whole person—in our own culture, the formulas "gesundheit" and "God bless you" which many people automatically utter when they hear someone sneeze are vestiges of a time when this violent expulsion of breath was thought to be an ill omen. So in some cultures, to utter one's own name with one's outgoing breath was thought to imperil the soul. When Ishi, last of the Yahi Indians, wandered out of the Sierra Nevada foothills in 1911, he never revealed his true name, so he was called Ishi, which he had said meant "man" in the Yahi language. Ishi took this to be his new name, and he himself never uttered it again.

In the Western tradition, too, we find many examples of the power over a person that comes with knowing his name. In a fairy tale, the gnomish Rumplestiltskin is going to take away a young queen's firstborn child unless she can say his name in three guesses. The queen is saved only because one of her men happens to overhear this little man with the improbable name gloating in a remote forest glen, "She'll never guess my name is Rumplestiltskin!" A more mundane example from our own century is the uneasiness we feel when an anonymous telephone caller, perhaps soliciting for a charity or trying to sell life insurance, addresses us by name. And of course, once your name is on a mailing list, you are prey to all sorts of indignities. These contemporary examples are anything but magical, but they illustrate the same basic attitude toward the name. There is a bit of slang, probably familiar to most of us from Westerns, by which *handle* means *name,* as in "What's your handle, pardner?" Even if the primary meaning of *handle* here is that by which a person may be grasped conceptually, we unconsciously think also of something to hold on to, to manipulate. This is the power of the name again.

The conscious or unconscious feeling that uttering a name can evoke the person or thing named is very strong. One of the most widespread customs stemming from this belief is a taboo on speaking of the dead by name, which is found in cultures all over the world. Ghosts are feared in cultures all over the world too, and this taboo on uttering the names of the dead arises from a desire not to summon the ghost of the person whose name was spoken, not to call the ghost's attention to the living. The Indians of California sought to sever all the ghost's ties with the world of the living, usually by burning or burying the possessions of the dead. Sightings of a ghost were often attributed to some possession of the deceased which had inadvertently not been destroyed. Similarly, they ceased to refer to the dead person by name. Just as a physical object is destroyed by burning or burial, a name is destroyed by not uttering it.

Customs spawned by the evocative power of the name are evident in our own culture too. We once had a belief that to name the Devil was to summon him, which gave rise to expressions like "Old Nick" by which we could refer to the Devil without having him put in an unwanted appearance. Even today, when we are talking about someone and he suddenly shows up, we may still say, "Speak of the devil . . ." Even the old joke about whispering "vermouth" over gin to make a really dry martini plays on the power of the name.

A negative example of the evocative power of the name is the ever-increasing use of euphemistic expressions today. An exaggerated consciousness of projecting a favorable public image motivates many of these euphemisms, but they also try to mask unpleasant realities by using emotionally neutral words. It is innocent enough to call a house trailer a "mobile home," or to put up a sign in front of the dump that says "refuse disposal site" or "sanitary landfill," but some euphemisms are dangerous. George Orwell points this out in a trenchant essay "Politics and the English Language." When we call a slum the "inner city," we don't feel any responsibility toward it; when we call the children of ethnic minorities "culturally deprived," we deny that they have a culture of their own; and when we call armed soldiers a "peacekeeping force," we are deluding ourselves that violence begets peace. In all of these cases, we are using the power of the word to whitewash reality instead of responding to its challenges.

People everywhere seem to feel, consciously or unconsciously, that uttering a name can evoke the thing named. By extension, we feel that talking about something can make it happen, or at least make it more likely to happen. For example, if you have a gopher problem in your garden and the gophers have ravaged the corn and decimated the carrots, you feel that you are tempting fate to say, "Well, at least they've left the tomatoes alone." Otherwise, if you went out the next day and found your tomato plants destroyed, you might not even be surprised. This sort of thing happens just often enough that we can't altogether banish from our minds the nagging suspicion that we are asking for trouble to speak of unpleasant possibilities. In more serious situations, we feel uneasy in mentioning unpleasant possibilities at all. In the case of critical illness, or in discussing life insurance policies, for example, death is often alluded to only vaguely, as in "If anything happens to your husband . . ." Because of the old saying that "accidents come in threes," miners are sometimes reluctant to discuss a mining accident for fear that mentioning one may precipitate two more.

If we believe that talking about things, especially unpleasant things, can make them happen, we also believe that other words can keep them from happening. For example, the gardener who tempts fate by mentioning gophers and tomatoes in the same breath might preface his remark with, *"I shouldn't say this,* but the gophers have left the tomatoes alone." There are also common verbal formulas which we can invoke to avert the misfortune that we might otherwise be asking for if we speak of it. In trivial cases we can say, "The gophers have left the tomatoes alone, *knock on wood,"* and in more serious matters there are variants of "If anything should happen to your husband, *heaven forbid . . ."* In Yiddish, the formula *kenahura,* meaning "no evil eye," is invoked to protect the speaker who mentions unpleasant possibilities, as in "I haven't had a cold for three years, *kenahura."* This formula can also be appended to compliments and other expressions of good fortune, so that there is no danger of tempting fate by saying how well things are going. This is the reverse psychology aspect of word magic, akin to the notion that it will rain if you wash your car or forget your umbrella. By this same reverse psychology, people don't wish an actor good luck as he goes on stage; with the best of intentions they say, "Break a leg!"

If the word of an ordinary human being is thought to have an effect, then how much more so the word of

circle of light by a vast sunless sea; they commanded "Earth!" and instantly land appeared in the midst of the waters. The word may bring the gods themselves into being. In an ancient Egyptian myth, Thoth creates the other lesser gods by pronouncing their names, and in a different Egyptian account of creation, Khepri, the first god, creates himself by uttering his own name. God's command in Genesis, "Let there be light," and the opening verse of the Gospel of John, "In the beginning was the Word," introduce this theme in the Judeo-Christian tradition. The power of the divine word is proclaimed when the Lord says, speaking through Isaiah, "As surely as rain and snow that fall from heaven return not there, but water the earth that it yield seed for the sower and bread for the hungry, so my Word that goes forth from my mouth shall not return unto me in vain; it shall accomplish what I desire and carry out that for which I dispatched it."

But even if the word of the gods is potent, the gods themselves are still subject to the power of the name. We find a recurrent belief that the gods can be coerced to do the bidding of anyone who calls them by their real names. This belief was very widespread in the ancient Western world, and it is alive today in the Middle East, for example, where it is thought that the jinn must answer and obey the person who has discovered their secret names. The Kabbalists of medieval Judaism believed that knowledge of the names of the angels could give one control over the forces of nature. In a powerful ancient Egyptian myth, Isis made herself an immortal goddess by learning the secret name of the sungod Ra. Isis was a sorceress; she fashioned a serpent which bit Ra, and as the poison began to afflict him Isis said, "Tell me your name, for the man shall live who is called by his name." Ra told Isis all his lesser names, but the poison only burned hotter in him, until at last he revealed to her the secret name which had been hidden in his breast since his birth. With the knowledge of this name, Isis became queen of the gods.

This theme appears in the Judeo-Christian tradition too, in the belief that to utter the name of God is to invoke God's presence. The Hebrews felt a strong bond between word and deed, between utterance and causation, and it is no accident that the Old Testament often refers to the name of God as if to God himself: "Beware of him [an angel of the Lord] and obey his voice, ... for my name is in him"; "They that know thy name will put their trust in thee"; "The name of the Lord is a strong tower." The Old Testament is quite circumspect about referring to God by the holy name revealed to Moses, *Yahweh* or *Jehovah;* usually the substitute *Adonai,* "Lord," appears. In fact, in reading the scriptures aloud, Jews say *Adonai* even where the text reads *Yahweh.* Taking the name of the Lord in vain—invoking him for some profane or trivial purpose—was one of the most serious offenses in Old Testament times.

The New Testament speaks frequently of the "name of Jesus." Paul exhorts us, for example, "Whatsoever ye do in word or deed, do all in the name of the Lord Jesus." This was clearly no mere formulaic convention in the eyes of the early Christians. In the Gospel of John, Christ repeats in various ways, "Whatsoever ye shall ask in my name, that I will do." And he assures us explicitly that invoking his name invokes his presence, when he says, "Where two or three are gathered together in my name, there am I in the midst of them."

Judaism and Christianity are not alone among the world's major religions in stressing the power of the divine name. We find the same emphasis in Islam too, where the invocation *bismillah,* "in the name of Allah," is often on the lips of devout Muslims. Hinduism and Buddhism, too, hold that the divine name has the power to evoke the divine presence. Hinduism, in fact, goes on to say explicitly that the name of God is not a mere word but a spiritual force. One sage of modern India, Swami Ramdas, fully within the mainstream of orthodox Hindu thought, tells us that the name is not a symbol for God; the name *is* God.

In still other traditions, the supreme reality is symbolized by some simple but powerful epithets devoid of personal or anthropomorphic overtones. These symbols may appeal to those who find themselves unresponsive to more familiar and traditional terms for the ultimate reality. Philosophers have called it "the Absolute" or sometimes simply "Being." Jewish mystics have called it *Ein-Sof,* "the Infinite," and to some, such as the Greek mystic Plotinus, it is simply "the One." In Chinese mysticism, the ultimate reality is summed up in one pregnant word *Tao,* "the Way."

Many adherents of the world's major religions put the power of the holy name into practice through the repetition of spiritual formulas containing a holy name or a divine attribute. Depending on the tradition, these formulas may be repeated a fixed number of times a day, or at fixed hours, or at any time; they might be repeated just in ritual situations, or in moments of stress—to overcome fear, for example—or as often as possible throughout the day. In the Catholic tradition, millions repeat the Hail Mary daily, while an anonymous medieval English mystical document called *The Cloud of Unknowing* recommends the repetition of a very simple word like *God* or *love.* These words are combined in a formula dear to Protestants, *God is love.* But the holy name that is dear to all Christians is simply *Jesus,* as attested eloquently, for example, in the Protestant hymn which begins, "How sweet the name of Jesus sounds in a believer's ear."

In the Eastern Orthodox tradition, the Prayer of Jesus—"Lord Jesus Christ, Son of God, have mercy on me"—has been used since the days of the Desert Fathers in the Sinai peninsula in the early centuries of the Christian era. There is a considerable body of literature on the use of this formula as a meditative technique. In Judaism, among the best-known of spiritual formulas are *Barukh attah Adonai,* "Blessed art thou, O Lord," *Shema Yisrael Adonai Elohenu Adonai Ehad,* "Hear, O Israel, the Lord our God, the Lord is one," and *Adonai, Adonai, El Rahum ve-Hannun,* "Lord, Lord, merciful and compassionate," which has an almost exact parallel in one of the best-known of Islamic formulas, *Bismillāh ir-Rahmān ir-Rahīm,* "In the name of Allah, the merciful, the compassionate." Other formulas in Islam are *Allāhu akbar,* "God is great," *Lā ilāh ill' Āllāhu,* "There is no god but God," and simply *Allāh,* "God."

In the Hindu tradition, there are a great many of these spiritual formulas, since the one supreme reality is loved and worshipped in many forms and under a great many names. Such a formula is called a *mantra* or *mantram*. *Mantra* is the term more widely known in the West, but *mantram* is the original Sanskrit form of the word, which is pronounced as if it were spelled "mun-trum" in English. The etymology of *mantram* sheds some light on the power of the word. It comes from the Sanskrit root *man,* "to think," plus a suffix *-tra* which denotes agent or instrumentality, so *mantram* could be understood as implying something like "tool for the mind."

Mantram is sometimes unfortunately translated as "incantation," perhaps because in Hindu mythology and even in Hindu and Buddhist folklore certain mantrams are supposed to have miraculous powers of curing snakebites, bringing rain, and so forth. But "incantation" is a misleading translation. The mantram is essentially a holy name, a name of God or a formula symbolizing the ultimate reality. It is used by devout Hindus and Buddhists just as devout Christians and Jews and Muslims use their spiritual formulas, which in this context may well be called mantrams too: all are used as a focus for devotion, as a means of steadying the tense or troubled or agitated mind, and as a constant reminder of the presence of God. More than that, mystics in all these traditions testify that the mantram, systematically repeated over a period of years, can permeate our consciousness, transforming our character and enabling us to rise to the highest state of spiritual awareness.

This is a tremendous claim, and one which we are naturally sceptical of in our times, sometimes even if we have been born into a tradition in which the holy name is used. Yet nowhere do we find stronger confirmation of the power of the word than in the twentieth-century West. Folklore, myth, and scripture, language and daily customs, all attest our deep-seated faith that words have power, and this is not just superstition. The word can mold our thinking and influence our behavior in a very real way, as every speech writer and advertising agent knows.

Enormous sums are spent annually on advertising, and evidently it pays off. Manufacturers carefully choose a catchy name for their product, a name which ideally combines snappiness, novelty, and aptness. "Crunchy" sounds good in the name of a breakfast cereal, for example, but its connotations are unfortunate for a line of compact cars. This catchy name is often embedded in a jingle which is catchier still, and such a union of word, tune, and rhythm can stick in our minds with an amazing tenacity. But the real key to advertising success is insistent repetition. The advertiser keeps hammering away at us, repeating his message, and finally it gets into our minds. Then, without understanding why, we find ourselves buying things we do not need, or even things which we know are dangerous to our health. We may think we are acting as free agents, but the advertiser is under no such delusion; to him it is the response to the word planted deep in our minds that makes us buy.

If an external agent can use the power of the word

to manipulate our thought and behavior like this, and with enormous success, we can choose to put this power to more positive use for ourselves, too. In the 1920s a French psychologist advocated repeating the phrase "Day by day in every way I'm getting better and better" as a means of self-improvement. Here again we see repetition as the key to getting something into our minds. In the hope that they really would get better, many people followed his advice, and no doubt it did actually brighten their outlook and enhance their self-confidence. But "Day by day in every way I'm getting better and better" could not have had a profound psychological impact, because it does not appeal to what is deepest in us. On the other hand, this is exactly why anyone can respond to the mantram, the holy name, whatever his religious convictions or lack of them, because it does appeal to what is deepest in us in words charged with power, which repetition drives deep into our mind. So the mantram is not something occult or impractical, and it is not something which appeals only to those from the East; we can all respond to the mantram and benefit from it.

In the pages that follow, Eknath Easwaran presents a clear exposition of the mantram's power to transform us. His approach is direct, practical, and not without humor. Above all, it is uniquely open to everyone, no matter what their background. Although his outlook is universal, Easwaran's background is Hindu; he grew up in a large joint family in the matrilineal tradition of Kerala state, South India, and he regards his mother's mother, the head of his ancestral family, as his spiritual teacher. He began the study of Sanskrit at an early age, and from his grandmother he absorbed the best of the rich spiritual heritage of India. As he grew up, Easwaran also immersed himself in English literature, and eventually he became chairman of the Department of English at the University of Nagpur, where he was deeply devoted to his students. Through the guidance and the personal example of his grandmother, Easwaran had already come to base his life on spiritual values, and soon after arriving in this country on the Fulbright exchange program in 1959 he began giving talks on meditation and the spiritual life. In 1960 he established the Blue Mountain Center of Meditation in Berkeley to carry on his work of teaching meditation.

In commenting on the scriptures and interpreting the writings of the great mystics of all religions, Easwaran does not rely on scholarship, but on his own experience in meditation and his personal practice of the spiritual life. As a family man, he tells us that the spiritual life is not one of withdrawal from the world. It is an active life which seeks to make a real contribution to the solution of the many problems that face the world today, while not forgetting that to transform others we must first transform ourselves. This presentation of the mantram is rich with details which show a penetrating observation of daily life in twentieth-century America, and it shows incisive insight into the workings of the mind. The appeal is pragmatic: Easwaran invites us to try using the mantram ourselves and see what its benefits are. He presents some of the world's great mantrams and gives detailed instructions in how and when to repeat the mantram as an effective means of gaining some mastery over the mind. The use of the mantram is then set against the larger background of the body of spiritual disciplines common to all the great religions of the world, especially the practice of meditation.

RICHARD B. APPLEGATE

Department of Anthropology
Sonoma State College

What the Mantram Is ❀

When I was a child, growing up in Kerala state, South India, I used to wake up every morning in our spacious ancestral home to the sweet sound of my Grandmother singing her mantram as she swept the courtyard with her coconut fiber broom:

Haré Rāma Haré Rāma,
Rāma Rāma Haré Haré,
Haré Krishna Haré Krishna,
Krishna Krishna Haré Haré.

At that time I don't suppose I gave the mantram much thought; it was just something I heard every morning from the lips of someone I loved very deeply. Only much later, when I began to face the storms that life is full of, did I remember my Grandmother's unshakable strength and begin to repeat her mantram myself. Since then, every day has brought a deeper realization of the mantram's power to turn fear into fearlessness, anger into compassion, and hatred into love.

I grew up in a Hindu family, but all the great religions have produced powerful spiritual formulas like this which are the highest symbol of the Lord. In the Catholic tradition, and many other traditions in both East and West, such a formula is called the Holy Name; in Hinduism and Buddhism, it is also called a mantram. Saint John refers to the Holy Name, to the mantram, when he declares: "In the beginning was the Word, and the Word was with God, and the Word was God." A very simple and devoted man of God, Swami Ramdas, whom my wife and I had the blessing of meeting in India, tells us very much the same thing when he says, "the Name *is* God." In remembering the name of the Lord, by whatever name we call him, we are remembering the Lord himself.

The mental repetition of the Holy Name is one of the simplest and most effective ways of practicing the presence of God, to use the medieval French mystic Brother Lawrence's phrase. It is absolutely practical, and it can appeal to our common sense. When we repeat the mantram, we are not hypnotizing ourselves, or woolgathering, or turning our back on the world. Repetition of the mantram is a dynamic discipline by which we can transform all that is negative in us in order to make our greatest possible contribution to the welfare of those around us.

The Lord has been called by many names in different lands and different ages, but by whatever name we call, we are calling on the same Lord of Love, the same ultimate Reality. This is the message declared everywhere by those rare men and women who have had the daring and the resoluteness to give everything to realize the Lord, to see him in the very depths of their consciousness and simultaneously in all those around them. This experience of the indivisible unity of life is one and the same everywhere, but men and women of God tailor their message to suit the needs and temperament of their time, just as I speak English to my friends in this country and my mother tongue, Malayalam, to my mother. Great figures on the spiritual path, like Jesus the Christ, Moses, the Compassionate Buddha, or Mohammed, have all given us the same message: "Live only for yourself and you will never grow; live for the welfare of all those around you and you will grow to your full stature." The message is the same; only the idioms differ.

So in each tradition we have a different Holy Name, a different mantram, but all are equally valid. Many different languages are spoken in India, and in train stations travelers will hear water venders calling out "vellam" in my old state of Kerala, "tanni" in the neighboring state of Tamil Nadu, "nilu" further north in Andhra, and "pani" in Hindi-speaking areas. Since I come from Kerala, I respond to "vellam": to me, it sounds the most like water of all these words. But to you who speak English, "water" sounds just right. Whatever the name, it is the same water; it is equally refreshing by any name, and it quenches our thirst just as well.

I have no quarrel with different labels and different approaches to the spiritual life. If the Lord is Christ to you and you respond deeply to Jesus the Christ, well and good; if you call the Lord Allah, or Krishna, or the Divine Mother, well and good. I don't even get agitated when people tell me that they don't believe in God at all. Usually they are thinking of something external, some extraterrestrial being swinging between Neptune and Pluto. When I use the word *Lord,* I am not referring to anything separate from us, but to the Divine Ground of existence of which we are all part. The Lord is the supreme Reality which is the very core of our being, ever pure, ever perfect. He is our real nature, my real me, your real you. So when people tell me they don't believe in God, I simply ask them, "Do you believe in yourself?" "Of course," they say. "Then," I reply, "you *do* believe in God." Such people still respond to the supreme Reality, whether they call it the Clear Light or collective consciousness or whatever else they prefer. I had an English friend on the Blue Mountain in South India who used to be allergic to the word *God* or *Lord;* he always spoke of "Nature with a capital *N*." So when he would ask me how my mother's health was, I used to tell him, "She is doing very well, thanks to the grace of Nature with a capital *N*." We are all speaking the same language.

So whatever religion you profess, or if you profess no religion, you can still use the mantram. In a book applying some of the techniques of meditation to medical problems, a well-known doctor from this country suggests using the word *one* as a mantram. The author's intent was to avoid any reference to religion altogether, which is not inappropriate, since meditation is a technique rather than a religion. But as I read his suggestions I thought, "Aha, he can't get off that easily." In the most ancient Hindu scriptures, God is said to be *advaita,* "One without a second"; Plotinus, the great Christian mystic of the third century, calls the Godhead simply "the One," and the beautiful Jewish confession of faith, the Shema, begins, "Hear, O Israel; the Lord thy God, the Lord is one."

The mantram is the living symbol of the profoundest that the human being can conceive of, the highest that we can respond to and love. When we repeat the mantram in our mind, we are reminding ourselves of this supreme Reality enshrined in our hearts. It is only natural that the more we repeat the mantram, the deeper it will sink into our consciousness. As it goes deeper, it will strengthen our will, heal the old divisions in our consciousness that now cause us conflict and turmoil, and give us access to deeper resources of strength, patience, and love to work for the benefit of those around us.

"The mantram becomes one's staff of life," declares Mahatma Gandhi, "and carries one through every ordeal. It is repeated not for the sake of repetition, but for the sake of purification, as an aid to effort . . . . It is no empty repetition. For each repetition has a new meaning, carrying you nearer and nearer to God."

There is nothing miraculous about this. When you repeat the Holy Name you are calling on the Lord in your own heart, and he will give you access to your own deeper resources. This is not something you do for two minutes one day and then give up because no results are immediately forthcoming, although even a little repetition of the mantram is helpful. If you call on the Lord long enough and sincerely enough, he cannot help responding. I saw a graphic illustration of this once when my wife and I were walking in Berkeley near the campus and chanced upon the final scene of a lover's quarrel. The young lady must have given her boyfriend his hat, told him that she never wanted to see him again, and pushed him out the door. He stood there on the sidewalk and began to call her name: "Cynthia, Cynthia." He shouted it louder and louder and soon the whole block was echoing with "Cynthia! Cynthia! Cynthia!" Passers-by were staring, the neighbors were coming out of their houses to see what was going on, and dogs began to howl. Finally Cynthia opened an upstairs window and told him, "All right, I'm coming down!" In just the same way, sincere and systematic use of the Holy Name can bring the power of the Lord to play in our own lives.

The popular etymology of the word *mantram* gives us some clue what it means to have the Holy Name at work in our consciousness. Although Sanskrit scholars may look askance, it is said that *mantram* comes from the roots *man,* "the mind," and *tri,* "to cross." The mantram is that which enables us to cross the sea of the mind. The sea is a perfect symbol for the mind. It is in constant motion; there is calm one day and storm the next. We see only the surface, with hardly any inkling of the strange creatures that lurk below or the tremendous currents that sweep through the depths. From where we stand on this shore, the far shore is so completely out of sight that we find it hard even to imagine that there *is* another shore.

Most of us are aware of the motion of the mind only on the surface level of consciousness, where our thoughts jump like grasshoppers from one thing to another. Stray observations on our surroundings, old memories, plans for the future, a rush of elation over some good news, regrets over the past, a line from a popular song, worries about our problems, physical sensations, resentments toward those around us, and a craving for something to eat, all follow one another in just a matter of minutes. In themselves, most of these thoughts are not actually harmful; a few of them might actually be rather elevating. The trouble is that we have very little control over them. If you ask the thoughts, they would say, "This poor fellow thinks he is thinking us, but *we* are thinking *him*."

Below the surface level of consciousness, what storms rage! Here are our deep-seated fears and hostilities, our cravings and conflicts. These are the deep divisions in our consciousness which make it difficult for us to concentrate, difficult to be loyal and steadfast. Often these divisions are at the root of serious physical ailments. They come to us in our sleep as nightmares, and all too often they plunge us into depression. Such storms sap our will and our vitality. The vast majority of us see no way to change this situation; we have come to accept it as inevitable, as part of human nature. But let me assure you that this is not our real nature; it is only our conditioning. Deep within us we have immense reserves of will, loyalty, patience, compassion, and love; it is only that we do not know how to unlock these resources and bring them into full play in our daily lives. But this is something all of us can learn to do, if we can gain control of our minds.

Control of the mind is something that has never occurred to most of us; to some it may even sound cold or rigid. Many people, especially those who are highly educated, feel that control would stifle the untrammeled freedom of their thoughts. But none of us question the need for control, for discipline, in mastering physical skills. Take eating, for example; it never even occurs to us what dexterity it requires simply to get food onto a fork and guide it to our mouths. Only when we see a baby learning to feed itself, getting more cereal on its face than in its mouth, do we realize that our effortless skill in eating comes from long years of practice. We have taught our hand to obey us. How would you feel if your hand suddenly refused to take orders from you, if it poured the coffee over your salad or fed you soup with the spoon upside down? This is exactly how we let our mind treat us, because we have never given it the proper training. When we want to concentrate, the mind generates a host of irrelevant worries and distractions. When we want to be dedicated, it brings in all sorts of conflicts and reservations. When we want to be loving, it drags out its little collection of trivial resentments and old hostilities. But when we learn to control the mind, to slow down its feverish pace, to welcome those thoughts we approve of and dismiss those that are negative, we will find what a sense of mastery this brings.

When most of us think of self-control, we think of something external. We may manage to keep from doing the wrong thing, but our mind is in turmoil; we may manage to keep from saying the wrong thing, but the words we're thinking are far from parliamentary. Here it is not enough to tell ourselves, "Keep a stiff upper lip, old boy," and put on a calm front. We can all have such control over the mind that calmness becomes our natural state. We can learn to turn our backs on our private satisfactions when necessary without a ripple of protest in the mind, and we can learn to function in the most trying circumstances without a trace of agitation. This is not control imposed from without; it is real mastery over our life.

The great mystics call this process calming or stilling the mind, and it means bringing every mental process under our complete control—not just on the conscious level, but in the unconscious too. For the vast majority of us, our will is operative only on the surface level. Most of us have little enough control even over our conscious mind, but the fears and hostilities and cravings that we are aware of are just the tip of the iceberg. In dreams and nightmares, we get some inkling of the strange world below the level of waking consciousness. Our fears and cravings are much strong at this level, and we have virtually no control over them. The deepest levels of the unconscious are completely beyond our awareness, yet it is here that our problems have their tap root. In the deeper unconscious, instead of the many small fears that we are aware of on the surface level—the fear of going bald, for example, or the fear of overdrawing our checking account—there is fear itself. And here too, bound up in our unconscious conflicts, fears, and cravings, is an immense reserve of creativity, wisdom, and love.

Of course, we cannot get at the unconscious directly. We have to strengthen our will gradually and learn to extend our conscious control over deeper and deeper levels of the mind. As our will grows, we transform and harness the negative forces in consciousness, which unlocks all our vast potential. Finally, when we have eliminated all barriers between the conscious and the unconscious, we are able to move about on any level of consciousness fully aware, with our will completely operative. Mahatma Gandhi assures us that we can come to have such effortless mastery over our mind that even in our dreams a selfish thought will not arise. This is what stilling the mind means: laying to rest permanently every negative and selfish force in consciousness.

There is a popular misconception that to still the

mind is to become a zombie or robot. It is just the opposite. The calmer and stiller the mind becomes, the more we can realize in our daily lives our true birthright of security, joy, and tireless energy to work for the welfare of those around us. Meher Baba, a well-known saint of modern India, used to say that a mind that is fast is sick, a mind that is slow is sound, and a mind that is still is divine. This is what the Bible means when it says, "Be still and know that I am God."

In comparing the mind to the sea, I often recall the walks my wife and I used to take every day around Lake Merritt in Oakland. Usually the wind ruffled the water, and all we could see was the surface. But on rare mornings when there was no wind and the lake was absolutely calm, we could see right down to the bottom. Similarly, when the mind is stilled, we become aware of the Lord of Love, who is enshrined in the very depths of our consciousness. This does not mean seeing visions or hearing voices; it means that we have had direct, immediate experience that all life is one. When we have had this experience, we will be incapable of doing anything that violates this unity of life, and we will live for the welfare of all.

If we can take advantage of all the opportunities for repeating the mantram throughout the day—while waiting, while walking, while falling asleep at night—

the mantram can help keep the mind calm and secure. When we are afraid, or angry, or driven by a strong urge for our own personal satisfaction at the expense of those around us, the mantram can transform these strong emotions into a source of tremendous positive power and help us refrain from acting or speaking impulsively. This is not repressing these powerful emotions; it is using them rather than letting them use us. The mantram has the power to turn fear into fearlessness, anger into compassion, and hatred into love.

People often tell me that this sounds too easy, too simple, too miraculous. In fact, this was my own reaction when my spiritual teacher, my mother's mother, suggested that I use the mantram to overcome stage fright. This was in my college days in India, when I was on the debating team. I went to my Grandmother and asked her what to do about the anxiety that used to grip me whenever I had to stand and speak before an audience. She told me not to dwell on the anxiety, but just to keep repeating the mantram instead. I was skeptical, but such was my love for my Grandmother that I tried it anyway. "I hope it works," I said, and the next time I sat on the platform waiting my turn to speak, I kept repeating the mantram in my mind. It seemed to help. Then I tried it on a few other occasions, and after a while I said, "I think it works." Now, after many years of using the mantram, I can assure you on the strength of my own personal experience, "I know it works."

I have heard people charge that repetition of the mantram is a kind of self-hypnosis. They believe that the mantram is just a string of nonsense syllables, or a word like any other word. "You might as well keep saying *hippopotamus* over and over again," they say, "or repeat the multiplication tables." Now, I'm willing to admit that repeating the multiplication tables would probably take your mind off your problems for a while, but the mantram is much more than something to keep your mind off your problems. The mantram is dynamic, powerful; it will sink deeper and deeper into your consciousness in a way that *hippopotamus* and the multiplication tables never can, because the mantram is the living symbol of the Lord. As it penetrates the deeper levels of consciousness it comes to stand for the highest we can conceive of, the highest we can aspire to, the highest we can love. At first we may just use the mantram to push thoughts aside, to keep worries from spinning around and around in our minds. But as the mantram takes root in our consciousness, it comes up under these thoughts and worries and cuts them off at the source. Then, when we have used the mantram for a long time with persistence and regularity, instead of just repeating it to keep our minds off worries *X, Y,* and *Z,* we can unlearn the habit of worry itself. Of course, this applies not just to worry but to all the negative thoughts and emotions that play in our minds, make us insecure, and drain our energy. The mantram is a dynamic tool for transforming all these into vitality, creativity, and love.

The power of the mantram may be demonstrated with a negative example, too. People might doubt that they would benefit from repeating *Jesus, Jesus, Jesus,* but who would question the harmful effects of repeating some very negative word like hate? If you sat for fifteen minutes repeating "hate, hate, hate," you would be the worse for it; yet this is just what we do when we keep dwelling on resentments. Correspondingly, if you sit for fifteen minutes repeating *Jesus, Jesus, Jesus,* or whatever mantram you respond to most deeply, you will be the better for it.

Advertising jingles and political slogans also demonstrate the power of the mantram. These too are short, simple formulas which can get into our consciousness and influence our behavior, just as the advertising copywriter intends. We hear the advertiser's mantram over the radio and on television, we see it on billboards and in the press, and before we are even aware, it has got into our minds. Then, when we walk into a store, the name on the box or on the can catches our eye, the jingle begins to play in our mind, and we are tempted to buy. I have heard it said that advertisers don't mind shocking us, even offending us, if only they can get the name of their product to stick in our minds. Here, others are using the power of the word to manipulate us, to make us buy things that we don't need or that might even be harmful to us. But with the mantram we all can put the power of the word to right use.

Repetition of the mantram is a tremendously powerful discipline, but it is only one of a larger body of spiritual disciplines which have come down to us in all the great religions. The purpose of these disciplines is not discipline for its own sake, but for the sake of gaining mastery over our life, for the sake of realizing in the depths of our consciousness the indivisible unity of life and translating this realization into the service of those around us. The foremost of these spiritual disciplines is meditation, but whether you are prepared to meditate or not, you can still derive great benefit from the mantram. As with any other discipline, the more you put into it, the more you get out of it. The more you use the mantram with regularity and dedication, the deeper it sinks into your consciousness.

After many years of practice, when you have made considerable progress towards gaining mastery over the mind, you may become established in the mantram. Then the mantram has become an integral part of your consciousness. You no longer have to make an effort to repeat it; it goes on repeating itself in the depths of your consciousness. The joy of this state has to be experienced to be described; it purifies the mind, brings us peace, and fills us with a quiet certainty that we are adequate to any challenge life may bring our way.

In the annals of Islamic mysticism we find a very precise exposition of the power of the Holy Name to transform us. "All the hundred and twenty-four thousand prophets were sent to preach one word. They bade the people say *Allah* and devote themselves to Him. Those who heard this word by the ear alone let it go out by the other ear; but those who heard it with their souls imprinted it on their souls and repeated it until it penetrated their hearts and souls, and their whole being became this word. They were made independent of the pronunciation of the word; they were released from the sound of the letters. Having understood the spiritual meaning of this word, they became so absorbed in it that they were no more conscious of their separate selves." Each one of us can become so absorbed in the mantram that we are no longer preoccupied with ourselves. When we have become aware of the unity of life, we will find our joy in contributing to the joy of those around us; we will find our fulfillment in helping those around us to grow.

Some Great Mantrams ❧

Most mantrams symbolize the personal aspect of
the Lord. Although the supreme Reality which we call
the Lord is present everywhere, throughout the vast
cosmos and in the heart of every living creature, he
has taken on a human form from age to age so that
we might see him and love him and be inspired by his
example. Two thousand years ago, in a humble stable
in Bethlehem, the Lord came to us as Jesus the Christ
and worked for us until his body was crucified. Five
hundred years before that he came as the Compassionate Buddha, a prince who turned his back on an earthly
throne to walk the dusty roads of ancient India, preach-
ing that our fulfillment lies in extinguishing our self-
will and learning to live for the welfare of all. Each
time a divine incarnation comes to us, it is not to
bring new truths or to establish a new religion, but to
remind us of what we have forgotten—that we are all
one, and that we must live in harmony with this unity

by learning to contribute to the joy and fulfillment of all.

For any Christian, the very name of Jesus is a great mantram, in which we are asking Jesus the Christ to help us to become more like him—full of wisdom, full of mercy, full of love. In my old state of Kerala—where, according to tradition, the Christian community was founded by the apostle Thomas himself—Indian Christians call on the Lord as Yesu Christu. In keeping with their Hindu surroundings, they may even add *Om* and use *Om Yesu Christu* as their mantram. In the Eastern Orthodox tradition, a Christian mantram known as the Prayer of Jesus has long been practiced: *Lord Jesus Christ, Son of God, have mercy on us.* This Holy Name is sometimes shortened to *Lord Jesus Christ.* The Desert Fathers, holy men living in the Sinai desert a few centuries after Christ, bequeathed us the Prayer of Jesus along with detailed instructions on how to use it, based on their personal experience passed from generation to generation. There is also a marvelous book called *The Way of a Pilgrim,* in which a humble, anonymous villager in Imperial Russia describes in simple and moving words how he came to use the Prayer of Jesus and how it transformed his consciousness.

In the Catholic tradition, *Hail Mary* may be used as a very powerful mantram, full of the infinite love of the Divine Mother for us, her wayward children. In India we say that as long as a child is playing contentedly with its toys beside the back door, the mother keeps busy inside. But eventually the child gets tired of the toys, throws them away, and gives one full-hearted, full-throated cry for its mother. Then she drops everything, rushes to the door, picks up the child tenderly, and comforts it. In just the same way, when you and I stop playing with our toys of pleasure and profit, power and prestige, and call for the Divine Mother with all our heart, she will reveal herself to us in the depths of our consciousness.

In the Hindu tradition, *Rāma* is one of the simplest, most powerful, and most popular of mantrams. This Holy Name comes from the Sanskrit root *ram,* "to rejoice"; *Rama* means abiding joy. When we repeat this mantram, we are reminding ourselves of the source of abiding joy deep within us, which is the Lord. It was through the ceaseless repetition of *Rama, Rama, Rama* that the very ordinary young man Mohandas Karamchand Gandhi transformed himself into Mahatma Gandhi, who managed to free India from the greatest empire the world has ever seen without firing a single shot.

Rama is the heart of many other powerful mantrams in India. One is the mantram of Swami Ramdas, *Om Sri Rām jai Rām jai jai Rām,* which I heard being chanted when my wife and I visited his spiritual community in South India many years ago. In practical language, this mantram means simply, "May joy prevail." With the repetition of this mantram, we are praying that the abiding joy in the very depths of our consciousness, which is the Lord, might prevail over all that is selfish in us and bring us the joy that comes with realizing the indivisible unity of life.

One of the best-loved mantrams in India, and one that is well known in the West too, combines three beautiful names of the Lord:

> *Haré Rāma Haré Rāma,*
> *Rāma Rāma Haré Haré,*
> *Haré Krishna Haré Krishna,*
> *Krishna Krishna Haré Haré.*

Rama, of course, is "he who fills us with abiding joy." *Krishna* means "he who draws us to him"; his pull is irresistible. *Hare* (pronounced "haray") is the vocative form of *hari,* "he who steals our heart." When the Lord sent us into this world, he stole our heart and then looked about for a suitable place to hide with it. "If I hide on the highest mountain," he said, "they will climb it and find me. If I hide in the atom, they will split it and find me. If I hide in the stars, they will spy me out with their telescopes." So the Lord hid in the last place we would ever look—in the very depths of our own consciousness. We all hear his call, we are all looking for him, but most of us don't know where to look. We go to Reno thinking he might be there; we look in the kitchen, in the bar, in the library, in the bank, in our record collection. But the Lord has stolen our heart, and we will never find lasting fulfillment in any of these places; we will find what we are really looking for only in the depths of our own consciousness, in the kingdom of heaven within.

Om namah Shivāya, a mantram that is especially popular in South India, is a supplication to the Lord as Shiva. In the Hindu Trinity, in which the principles of creation, preservation, and destruction are personified, Shiva is the destructive aspect of the Godhead, and in this mantram we are calling upon him to put an end to our selfishness, to our sense of separateness. This mantram reminds us that the Lord has a sterner side. He loves us all with infinite tenderness, but he is also prepared to make us suffer a little if suffering will teach us to make the wise choices in life which enable us to grow to our full stature.

It is one of the most bitter truths in life that pain often goes hand in hand with growth. On the physical level, for example, poor eating habits and too little exercise lead to all sorts of physical problems. If the resulting pain spurs us to change our way of living, then pain has helped us to grow. On the spiritual level,

59

when we live selfish lives based on the pursuit of our own private satisfactions, we suffer alienation from those around us; the nagging suspicion that we have not found real fulfillment will not give us any peace. If this suffering enables us to change our ways and learn to live for the welfare of those around us, then this suffering is the sign of the Lord's concern for our spiritual growth.

Om mani padmé hum is a great Buddhist mantram, which refers to the "jewel in the lotus of the heart." This jewel is the permanent treasure of joy and security hidden deep within us, waiting to be discovered. Here the heart is compared to a lotus, which is one of the most beloved of spiritual symbols in Hinduism and Buddhism. In the village in Kerala state in which I grew up, there were two beautiful lotus ponds. The lotus would grow up from the muddy bottoms of these ponds, but the mud would not stain its lovely, waxen petals. For this reason, the lotus is a perfect symbol of purity, reminding us that whatever mistakes we may have committed in the past, we can all purify our consciousness through systematic repetition of the mantram; our hearts can open with love and compassion for all.

In the Jewish tradition, *Barukh attah Adonai* means "Blessed art thou, O Lord." The Lord is the source of all strength, all courage, all joy, all love, and the greatest blessing we can know is to realize him in the depths of our consciousness and gain access to these deeper resources, which the Lord will magnify in us for his service. When we see the Lord of Love in our own heart and become aware of the indivisible unity of life, this is the supreme blessing, not only for us, but for all those who come in contact with us.

Bismillāh ir-Rahmān ir-Rahīm is a beautiful Muslim mantram, meaning "In the name of Allah, the merciful, the compassionate." The Lord of Love, who is the source of all mercy and all compassion, has given us a wide margin to experiment with the playthings of life. The burden of past mistakes will fall away when we turn our eyes to the Lord, when we set our hearts on becoming united with him. Orthodox Muslims say this mantram before they speak, as a reminder that everything we say and everything we do should be in accord with the will of God, in accord with the indivisible unity of life.

These are all mantrams which call upon the personal aspect of the Lord. But the Lord has an impersonal aspect as well, which a few mantrams reflect. This impersonal aspect has been called by many formidable-sounding names: the Unmanifested, the transcendental Godhead, the ultimate Reality, the Absolute, Brahman. All these names are inadequate, because the underlying Reality of existence is beyond name and form, beyond time and space, beyond cause and effect. Jesus taught us to pray to our Father in heaven, Sri Ramakrishna in nineteenth-century Bengal worshipped the Lord as the Divine Mother, and Sufi mystics in the Islamic tradition call upon the Beloved, but there were sages in ancient India who did not refer to the Lord as either *he* or *she;* for them the ultimate Reality was *it* or *that*.

The perfect symbol of the impersonal aspect of the Godhead is the syllable *Om*. In Hinduism and Buddhism, many mantrams based on the personal aspect of the Lord begin with *Om,* so that a single mantram symbolizes the Lord as both personal and impersonal, as both manifest and unmanifest.

To explain why *Om* is such a perfect symbol of the impersonal Godhead, it is necessary to refer to a theory in the ancient Hindu scriptures which has much in common with recent discoveries in modern science. According to this theory, the entire phenomenal world consists of vibrations, just as matter, according to modern physics, may be looked at as a concentration of energy. The physicist will tell you that in the last analysis, this book is not a solid object; it is a structure of vibrating energies temporarily fixed in a particular pattern. In the Hindu theory of vibration, matter is the most rigid, the most "condensed" of vibrations; it is solid and perceptible to the senses. Energy is less

rigid, more subtle. It is not solid and often not perceptible, but it is not different in kind from matter; it is
still patterns of vibration, only in a more subtle state.
The subtlest of vibrations, according to the ancient
sages, is the so-called cosmic sound, the creative Word
out of which the entire universe of stars and seas,
plants and animals and human beings has evolved. The
passage from Saint John with which we began this
book—"in the beginning was the Word, and the Word
was with God, and the Word was God"—has an almost
exact parallel in the Rig Veda, one of the oldest of
Hindu scriptures, which speaks of the unmanifested
Godhead, called Brahman: "In the beginning was
Brahman, with whom was the Word, and the Word
was truly the supreme Brahman."

This Word, the cosmic sound, is not perceptible
to the senses, but it can be experienced in very deep
meditation. It is most closely approximated by the
syllable *Om*—or *Aum,* as it is sometimes pronounced.
When we utter *Om* with awareness of its significance,
we are to some degree evoking the supreme Reality
for which it stands.

Once a man and woman who had been meditating
under my guidance for a short while came to me and
said that they had been hearing the cosmic sound.
Their meditation was not likely to have been so very
deep, so to get to the root of the matter I went to their

home one morning to meditate with them. It turned out that they had been hearing the hum of the refrigerator. The real experience of the cosmic sound, as attested by mystics from the East and West alike, is something profound. Saint Francis of Assisi, for example, described it as a music so sweet and so beautiful that had it lasted a moment longer, he would have melted away from the sheer joy of it.

In any case, whether you accept the theory of vibration or not, *Om* is still a magnificent symbol of the Lord. For thousands of years it has stood for the ultimate Reality—the transcendental Godhead beyond all names and forms, beyond all sects and all denominations.

Most of us, however, do not respond deeply to the impersonal aspect of the Lord as the ultimate Reality. I sometimes tease my friends by asking them how they would like to have an impersonal girlfriend, a transcendental boyfriend. She is unmanifested, so how can you gaze into her eyes? He is beyond time and space, so how can you hold his hand? What most of us need and want is a personal incarnation: a figure whom we can visualize, whom we can hear stories of, whom we can love and try to model ourselves after, whether we call him Christ, Krishna, or the Buddha. So most of the great mantrams of the world's religions center around these tremendous figures. Such mantrams help us to cultivate ever-deepening devotion to the Lord of Love in whatever form we seek him, and can assist us in becoming united with him in the depths of our consciousness.

These are some of the most widely used and best-loved mantrams in the great religious traditions of the world, but there are many other names too by which men and women through the ages have called on the Lord for strength and support. Saint Francis of Assisi used to repeat "My God and my all" to help transform himself from Francis the would-be troubadour into Francis the instrument of God's love. And in the Hindu tradition, there are magnificent hymns called *The Thousand Names of the Lord* and *The Thousand Names of the Divine Mother,* which give us a vast selection of beautiful Holy Names. But many mantrams, especially in Hinduism or Buddhism, come out of a complex tradition whose references may be too elusive for us. Such mantrams are not likely to evoke a deep response in those who were not brought up in these traditions. So I stress those mantrams which are short, simple, and powerful, which come out of a long, established tradition and have carried many devoted men and women safely across the tempestuous sea of the mind.

Choosing a Mantram

Exercise some care in your choice of a mantram. It is important to take into account your own religious background, your response to the meaning, and the practical significance of the words. Choose a mantram from one of the established traditions, a mantram recommended by a spiritual teacher with personal experience of its power. Then, once you have chosen a mantram, do not change it.

There are two schools where the choice of a mantram is concerned. In what I playfully call the cloak-and-dagger school, you are taken into a little room, the light is switched off, and a voice whispers in your ear, "Here is your mantram. Don't reveal it to a soul." This is one way, and there are people who respond to it; it is the right way for them, and I have no quarrel with it. But there is another school of thought which is a little more my style, represented by a great mystic of South India named Ramanuja.

When Ramanuja was a spiritual aspirant, just beginning on the spiritual path, he was given his mantram by a very orthodox teacher who told him, in the orthodox manner, "Don't breathe a word of this to anybody." Ramanuja didn't see what all the mystery was about, and he asked, "What will happen if I *do* reveal my mantram to someone else?" His teacher told him, "Everyone who hears it will get the benefit, but you will be barred from salvation." When Ramanuja heard this, he went straight to the temple, climbed to the top of the highest tower, and called everyone in the village. "I know a mantram which will make you all secure and selfless," he told them, and he shouted his mantram again and again for everyone to hear. When his spiritual teacher heard about this, he pretended to be angry and scolded Ramanuja severely. But Ramanuja replied calmly, "If my damnation can alleviate the suffering of so many, it is a very small price to pay." It was an answer that pleased his teacher greatly.

This approach is one which the Buddha would call "the way of the open hand." The spiritual teacher says, "I don't have a closed fist; my hand is open. Everything I know that can help you cross the sea of life is yours for the asking; you can select the mantram that suits you best." But there is a responsibility which goes along with this approach: you must choose your mantram wisely, according to your deepest needs. If you respond deeply to Jesus, then *Jesus, Jesus* is the right mantram for you. If you respond deeply to the Divine Mother as the Virgin Mary, then *Hail Mary* is the right mantram for you. If you respond deeply to the Lord as the source of abiding joy, *Rama, Rama* is the right mantram for you.

You may respond to a mantram because of your childhood background, but there is a danger here, too; some people are allergic to particular names for the very same reason. Here I get very practical. If it is going to take a number of years of repetition just to make you like the mantram, and then more years to make the mantram part of your consciousness, it is a matter of simple economy to choose a mantram about which you have no reservations. So if you have difficulties with the mantram appropriate to your background, you might use *Rama, Rama* or the Buddhist mantram *Om mani padme hum,* which makes no direct reference to God at all.

Be wary of choosing a mantram *just* because it's exotic. The name of Allah may conjure up visions of date palms and camels with tinkling bells; this appeals to some people, and they say, "*Allah, Allah* is the mantram for me." The trouble with this kind of appeal is that after a few weeks, date palms begin to cloy, and you find yourself wanting to change to some other mantram.

I wouldn't suggest making up your own mantram, either. More than once I have had rugged individualists come to me and say, "I'd like to use *peace, peace, peace* as my mantram." *Peace* is a beautiful word, I agree, but not just any word will do as a mantram. Let me urge you to use a mantram of proven power, one which has enabled many men and women before you to realize for themselves the unity of life. The roots of such a mantram are far deeper than we can know when we first begin to use it, and this is what enables it to grow in our consciousness.

Use a mantram recommended by a spiritual teacher; you can be sure that it will be charged with the teacher's own personal experience of the mantram's power. All of the mantrams which I have mentioned here are mantrams of proven power, bequeathed to us by the great spiritual teachers of many traditions.

If no one mantram appeals to you more than any other, I would recommend *Rama, Rama,* one of the oldest, simplest, and most powerful of mantrams. Often, people who have found themselves unresponsive to other mantrams have protested that *Rama* does not mean anything to them either. It may be a while before the mantram "takes," so don't feel disappointed if it doesn't send you into raptures the first time you repeat it. When you have used the mantram for a while, you'll see for yourself what a difference it can make in your life. People who have begun to use *Rama* on the strength of this advice—experimentally, so to say—usually tell me later, "You know, *Rama* really works."

Another caution which I would sound here is not to use the impersonal mantram *Om* by itself. I sometimes find people who do not respond to any of the mantrams centered around a personal aspect of the

Lord, such as *Jesus, Jesus.* When such people tell me that they would like to use *Om* as their mantram, I suggest instead that they choose one of the more personal mantrams which begin with *Om*; with such a mantram they are calling on both the personal and impersonal aspects of the supreme Reality we call the Lord. There is a good reason for this. People who feel great devotion to a personal incarnation like Jesus the Christ will naturally use his name as their mantram; that very devotion will drive the mantram deeper into their consciousness and release still more devotion. But those who would use an impersonal mantram will find that reaction against childhood associations or intellectual allegiance to the unmanifest Absolute is no substitute for devotion; it will not draw them on. *"Amor saca amor,"* Saint Teresa of Avila tells us: love draws out love. There is a deep vein of devotion in all of us if we can only tap it. So even for those who feel little devotion now, sustained use of one of the personal mantrams will bring devotion.

There is a delightful story which we tell in India to illustrate how the wise choice of a mantram takes our individual needs into account. A sage was once passing through a forest where a bandit had his hiding place. People for miles around were afraid of this bandit, and so he was surprised one day to see a stranger coming towards him so calmly, so full of security.

He strode up to the sage and asked, "Don't you know who I am?"

"Yes," the sage replied quietly, "you are the bandit everyone around here is afraid of."

Such quiet confidence caught the bandit off guard. "Then aren't you afraid of me?" he demanded. "Don't you know how terrible I am, how many people I have robbed, how many people I have killed?"

"All this robbing and killing is child's play," the sage replied. "Wouldn't you like a real challenge?"

"*What* real challenge?"

"I can show you an opponent far fiercer than any you have ever met, more resourceful and more treacherous than any you've taken on so far."

"Show me this opponent," the bandit said, all his enthusiasm roused. "I'll make mincemeat of him."

"It is your ego," said the sage, "your own sense of separateness. It will give you a fight that will test every ounce of your endurance."

The bandit hadn't counted on this. "My *what?*" he asked. "Where is it? How can I take it on?"

"Sit down, shut your eyes, and keep repeating *Rama, Rama, Rama,*" said the sage.

"I can't stand that name," said the bandit.

"Then what do you like?"

"Robbing and killing."

"Well, what do you like next after that?"

The bandit's face softened a little. "I like trees."

Now, I should tell you that this is a story I heard from my spiritual teacher, my mother's mother, and the word for tree is *mara* in my mother tongue. So the sage brightened and said, "You like trees, then? Well, just keep repeating *Mara, Mara, Mara.*"

The bandit didn't even answer; he was already absorbed in saying *Mara, Mara, Mara*—which, when you keep repeating it, becomes *Rama, Rama, Rama.*

The sage went off on his journey and gave little thought to this odd new disciple. A few months later, however, he happened to pass by the same spot and remembered the bandit whom he had instructed in the mantram. Where he had left his disciple, there was only an anthill—one of those huge anthills you see in the tropics. He broke the anthill open and inside was the former bandit, deeply immersed in awareness of the Lord. His delighted teacher gave him the name Valmiki, "he who found enlightenment in an anthill." This same Valmiki later composed the Ramayana, the great epic poem describing the deeds of the divine incarnation called Rama.

So no matter what the associations of your past, it is always possible to choose a mantram that can come to appeal to you deeply. Then, once you have chosen your mantram, do not change it. As one of the Desert Fathers, writing on the Prayer of Jesus, warns us with a homely image, a tree that is too often transplanted will not take root. Sri Ramakrishna tells us the same thing when he compares a person who keeps changing mantrams to a farmer who digs in ten different places looking for water. He starts digging for a while in one spot and goes on until the digging gets a little difficult. "The soil is too hard here," he says, and he goes somewhere else where the ground is softer. But soon it starts to cave in around his shovel, and he says, "It is too crumbly here." Then he goes elsewhere and digs until he hits a rock, and so he continues throughout the day. If he could put the same amount of time and energy into digging in one place, he would go deep enough to reach water, and his crops would flourish. It is exactly the same with the mantram. Don't lose heart if after three weeks you don't have spectacular results. It takes time, but once you have made the mantram an integral part of your consciousness, it will bear a rich harvest in joy, security, and a sense of unity with all life.

There have been people who hear my instructions on the mantram and go off full of enthusiasm repeating *Rama, Rama, Rama.* Then they come to me the next day and say, "Perhaps I would have been better off repeating *Jesus, Jesus, Jesus,* but I have been saying *Rama, Rama, Rama* for a whole day now." Let me assure you that using a mantram for one day doesn't commit you to that mantram for life, but within a reasonable period you should settle on the mantram which you feel suits you best. Then, no matter what happens, you will not need to change it again.

How to Say the Mantram

Instead of just saying the mantram once, the way we say hello at the beginning of a conversation, the idea is to repeat it over and over again, and to use every chance throughout the day for repeating it more. In all the great religions there have been mystics who have become so established in the mantram that they would be plunged into a deeper level of consciousness by hearing the Holy Name just once. But this is not likely to happen when we are just beginning to use it. The effect of the mantram is cumulative: constant repetition, constant practice is required for the mantram to take root in our consciousness and gradually transform it, just as constant repetition makes the advertiser's jingle stick in our minds. This may sound tedious, but it is far from that. The mantram soon becomes an old, familiar friend of whom we never grow tired.

The mantram is most effective when we say it silently, in the mind, with as much concentration as possible. A mantram is more than just a word or phrase; it is a force, and in order for this force to heal the divisions in our consciousness and to give us access to our deeper resources, it must be working from deep inside. At first, of course, we will be repeating the mantram only at the surface level of the mind. But if we repeat it with regularity and sustained enthusiasm, it will take root deep in our consciousness until it becomes as natural to us as breathing.

There is nothing mysterious about this process. We all have the capacity to concentrate, especially on things we like, and concentration itself is a deeper level of awareness. When we get absorbed in an intricate problem, or in reading our favorite author, or in listening to music we love, or in doing anything else that commands our full attention, we are no longer aware of our surroundings or of extraneous sights and sounds; we may not even be aware of our body. Our awareness of the external world is confined to the surface level of consciousness, and in moments of intense concentration, we experience a deeper level of awareness. It is just the same with the mantram; it can come from a level beyond awareness of sights and sounds, beyond awareness of the body, even beyond the level of words and conceptual thought.

Sometimes saying the mantram aloud a few times can help you get it started in the mind, and it is so rhythmical that it can be sung aloud, as it often is in all the great religions. Some of my friends even confess to singing it in the shower. But by and large I recommend repeating the mantram silently, and not dwelling on tune and rhythm and such matters. Anything which takes attention away from the mantram itself, such as counting, or worrying about intonation, or connecting the mantram with physiological processes, only weakens the mantram's effect; it is like trying to dive deep when you have an inner tube around your waist. So it is best right from the outset not to get dependent on external aids, not even the rosary that is used in many religious traditions. After a short while, any such aid is of little use, and eventually it will even hold you back. Counting or thinking about what your hands are doing only helps keep you on the surface level of awareness; it may even encourage your repetition to become mechanical. And let me urge you not to connect the repetition of the mantram with your breathing or your heartbeat. There is no harm if this happens of its own accord, but in making a conscious effort to link the mantram with these rhythms, you may interfere with vital processes which the body, with its native wisdom, is already regulating at optimum efficiency.

Sometimes, in the West as well as in the East, you hear that the mantram is only effective if repeated in a particular way—with exactly the right pronunciation and intonation, or a set number of times. Let me assure you that any way you say it, the Holy Name works. Whether you say it fast or slow, with an Oxford accent or a Tennessee drawl, for five minutes or for hours at a stretch, you are still repeating the name of the Lord of Love, who is waiting to be discovered in the depths of your consciousness.

If you are repeating the mantram with concentration, you need not think about the words themselves, either how they sound or what they mean. Sound and sense go together. Of course, it *is* important to know what your mantram means. I have sometimes heard the charge that a mantram is just nonsense syllables, mumbo-jumbo, but certainly no one would claim that *Lord Jesus Christ* or *Hail Mary* are nonsense syllables. So when people choose a mantram from a tradition they were not raised in—a Sanskrit mantram, for example—I always make sure that they understand its meaning and practical significance. But if you try to dissect the mantram, it will not come to life in your consciousness. Even reminding yourself what the mantram signifies as you repeat it does not help it sink in. What counts is with how much regularity you use the mantram, with how much sincerity and enthusiasm. It will take on deeper significance as your awareness deepens; as Gandhi says, each repetition has a new meaning, carrying you nearer and nearer to God.

Making the Mantram
a Part of Your Day ❦

You don't have to have set times to repeat the mantram; you can repeat it whenever you get a chance.
When you begin to look for opportunities to say the
mantram, you find them everywhere. If you get five
minutes at the post office, that is five minutes that you
can put to use repeating *Rama, Rama, Rama* or *Jesus,
Jesus, Jesus*. Later, while waiting for the bus, you
get five minutes more—or ten minutes, or maybe even
twenty. This is how you get time to say the Holy
Name, by becoming like a miser with all the little
moments you get throughout the day. You don't have
to wait for a stretch of two hours when no one is going
to disturb you; it will never happen. Every day you
pick up a few minutes here and a few minutes there,
and by the end of the year, as the bank advertisements
say, it all adds up.

The little waits and delays that life is so full of
are all opportunities to use the mantram. In the morning when you're waiting for the coffee to perk, you

can repeat the mantram instead of staring blankly at the wall. When you are standing in line at the bank, or the post office, or the supermarket, the mantram will make the wait seem shorter, and your example of calm and patience will help those around you too. When you are waiting for an interview, or for a test to begin, or for the doctor to come in, the mantram can save you a good deal of anxiety, which will lower your blood pressure and improve your performance. In all these cases you are putting your time to better use than if you were just letting your mind run on about what is troubling it. You are sending the mantram deeper into your consciousness, and often you are saving yourself from unnecessary tension and anxiety too.

Walking is one of the best times to repeat the mantram, especially if you walk briskly. The rhythm of your footsteps, the rhythm of the mantram, and the rhythm of your breathing all harmonize to soothe and invigorate the body and mind. This happens naturally, and there is nothing mysterious about it. Breathing is closely connected with our state of mind. People who are tense or angry breathe rapidly and irregularly; those who are calm, loving, and secure breathe like a little child, smoothly, slowly, and deeply. A brisk walk helps to make your breathing rhythm deep and even, and the mantram will help to calm your mind. So at work, try a mantram break: take a brisk five- or ten-minute walk repeating the mantram and see how much better you feel than if you had stayed at your desk with a cup of coffee. The mantram goes well with other rhythmical forms of exercise too, like jogging, swimming, or bicycle riding, but I especially recommend walking because it requires no special equipment, no special time, and you can keep it up right into the evening of your life.

You can make the mantram part of your daily routine in many other ways, too. For example, if you spend a lot of time reading or writing or typing, it is good to rest your eyes from time to time by looking up from your work and gazing into the distance. This is a perfect chance to use the mantram, and for people who are driven by their work, it is also a good exercise in detachment. If you find yourself working compulsively, just see how hard it is to drop your work for one minute to give your full attention to the mantram.

My friends and I shut our eyes and repeat the mantram silently for a moment before each meal. This reminds us that the food we are about to eat is a gift from the Lord, and that the energy it gives us should be used in the service of the Lord. This is especially helpful at lunch for people who are at work, away from the supporting circle of family and friends; at least once during the busy work day it is helpful to stop and remember the Lord within. If you are feeling tense and harried, with your stomach in knots and the gastric juices at war with one another, the mantram says, "All right, boys, break it up!" After all, mealtime is not the time to get involved in heated discussions or critical talk. A nourishing meal, cooked and served with love and eaten in the cheerful company of family or friends, is a sacrament, and the mantram is a beautiful way to begin it.

When you are sick or suffering any physical discomfort, the mantram is of great value. As more attention goes to the mantram, there is less attention for the physical sensations of discomfort or pain. Even seasickness is susceptible to this. When I was coming to this country by ship, we ran into a storm in the Indian Ocean which lasted for days. I had never been at sea before, and I must say that even blueberry waffles begin to lose their appeal when you're looking down into the sea one instant and staring up at the sky the next. One by one, even the most seasoned of my fellow passengers took quietly to the rails, but I just took to my mantram. One morning, towards the end of the storm, I walked into the dining hall for breakfast and found myself entirely alone in that vast room. I was able to do justice to a hearty breakfast, too. This impressed not only my fellow passengers but the crew also, and they were all asking me what kind of tablet I took. So when you have a headache or a toothache or any of the hundred and one other afflictions that can come our way, take an aspirin if you like, but be sure to say the mantram.

If you are really ill, instead of lying in bed watching television or solving crossword puzzles or just staring at the cracks in the ceiling, you can put this time to much better use by repeating the mantram. It will not only comfort you and take your mind off the pain; it can release curative forces from deep within. There is nothing occult about this. A good deal of the suffering involved in illness comes from dwelling on the symptoms, from worrying about how serious the illness is and when you will recover and how you will manage to carry on. This anxiety is what really impedes our recovery, and you can use the mantram to keep such worries from clouding your mind. In a mind that is at ease, the positive power of the mantram cannot help releasing the deep curative forces that are the body's natural and most effective measures for recovery.

The mantram goes well with any mechanical task that doesn't demand your full attention, especially if the task is rhythmic. You can repeat the mantram in your mind while washing dishes or polishing your shoes, while sweeping or sawing, or even while you are brushing your teeth. All too often when we are en-

gaged in mechanical tasks of this sort, the better part
of our attention is far from the job at hand. We may
be daydreaming or woolgathering—thinking about
yesterday, rehearsing what we would like to say to
our boss if we ever got the chance, letting some old
song run through our mind, dwelling on a pet worry
or resentment. Much more of our vitality than we sus-
pect ebbs out through this constant play of the mind.
We are deluding ourselves if we think that our minds
are always gainfully occupied, moving with clear
logical precision from premise to conclusion. When
we repeat the mantram while doing mechanical jobs,
we are not only sending the mantram deeper into our
consciousness; we are training our minds to stay in
the here and now.

Let me also add a word of caution about when
not to say the mantram. Some people can get so enthusiastic about the mantram that they get carried
away and repeat it when they should be devoting their
full attention to what they are doing. Do not try to
repeat the mantram when you are engaged in conversation, listening to instructions, reading or writing,
or listening to good music. Also, do not repeat it
when you are working at a potentially dangerous job—
say, one involving sharp tools or powerful machinery,
whether it is a big electric saw or just sharp knives in
the kitchen. That is the time to give your complete

attention to the job at hand. For the same reason, I do not recommend repeating the mantram while driving, especially in heavy traffic, because of the danger of getting absorbed in the mantram and not paying enough attention to the wheel, to your speed, to other cars, and to pedestrians and animals. Beyond this, it is up to each individual to decide what jobs are worthy of his or her full attention. A skilled carpenter may be able to say the mantram each time he swings his hammer. That is fine for him, but if I tried it, I have very little doubt that I would hit my thumb. So let each of us use his or her own judgment here.

The mantram can also be of great help when you have time on your hands. Boredom can be a real source of problems to people who don't know what to do with their time and attention. My wife and I used to walk around Lake Merritt in Oakland every morning, and I used to get fascinated at all the ways in which commuters would spend their ten or fifteen minutes while waiting for a bus to San Francisco. Many of them were smoking, not because they especially wanted to but because they didn't know what else to do with their time, and one chap, dressed to take on the bulls and bears on Montgomery Street, seemed intent on trying to drill a hole in the Oakland sidewalk with his umbrella. All of these people could have benefited greatly from the mantram. Most of us, in fact, do not realize how much of what we do is motivated simply by boredom, by restlessness, by not knowing what to do with our time. Here the mantram can save us a good deal of agitation and wasted energy, which we often court when we are bored by letting our minds run away with us.

Indiscriminate television watching is one sure sign of boredom. Friends of mine who work in hospitals tell me that many patients have the television going all day long, sometimes even with two sets both on in a single room, just because they do not know what else to do with their time. I would say, turn off the television, lie back, and repeat the mantram; the silence and the mantram will speed your recovery much more than *Queen for a Day*. I am particularly grieved when I hear of elderly people in retirement homes and convalescent hospitals parked in their wheelchairs in front of a blaring television set. I think, if only they had the mantram, what a good companion it would be for them. My mother, who is in her eighties and lives with me, devotes hours each day to the mantram. If she were asked—and if she could speak English—she would tell you without hesitation that she doesn't know the meaning of boredom.

For younger people who are active and healthy, of course, I am not suggesting nonstop repetition of the mantram in place of all the hours they now spend watching television. A grim statistic says that our children spend an average of over six hours a day in front of a television set, and adults are not far behind. When there is a good show, educational or wholesomely entertaining, let us watch, by all means, but otherwise we could invest these hours much more profitably. There are so many worthwhile activities that everyone in the family can participate in. We can walk or go swimming together; we can rediscover the lost art of conversation, getting to know our family and our friends and our neighbors better; we can devote a portion of our time to selfless causes which contribute to the welfare of all.

Then there are people who must always be reading something. At breakfast they read and reread what is written on the milk carton; on the bus going to work they pull out a novel or a crossword puzzle; when they go to clean the attic, they get caught by the old magazines piled in the corner. Wouldn't it be better to repeat the mantram than to go on reading everything in sight, just because it is there?

People who are compulsive talkers are not too different. There is an Arab proverb that each word we utter should have to pass through three gates before we say it. At the first gate, the gatekeeper asks, "Is this true?" At the second gate, he asks, "Is it necessary?" and at the third gate, "Is it kind?" If we applied this proverb strictly, most of us would have very little to say. I am not recommending silence, however, but control over our speech. Talk is good when it communicates, and cheerful, positive speech in moderation helps to maintain relations between family and friends. But those who are compulsive talkers can turn it to their advantage by repeating the mantram, and they can go a long way. Today it may be "Blah, blah, blah," but when the mantram finally takes hold, it will be "Rama, Rama, Rama." This is the way liabilities are turned into assets on the spiritual path.

One of the most important times to use the mantram is at night, when you are going to sleep. This is the time when all our problems come home to roost— all the turmoil of the day, all the anxieties of the following morning. This is why we have bad dreams, why we don't sleep very well and get up wishing we could sleep four hours more. So instead of falling asleep in your problems, put your book away, turn out the light, close your eyes, and begin repeating *Rama, Rama, Rama* or *Jesus, Jesus, Jesus* until you fall asleep in it. It takes some time and some effort to master this, but once you are able to fall asleep in the mantram, it will go on working its healing effect in your consciousness throughout the night.

Between the last waking moment and the first sleeping moment, there is an arrow's entry into the depths of your consciousness. This is one of the great discoveries in the unification of consciousness. It is a marvelous moment. You are neither awake nor asleep; you are between two worlds, and the tunnel is open. At that moment, you can send the mantram in just the way a bowler bowls a strike. You have seen how a good bowler picks up the ball and cradles it in his free hand, aims, and sends the ball rolling down the lane with just the right degree of spin to score a strike. It's very much like that with the mantram; you can learn to send the mantram right into the depths of your mind every night.

When this happens, you may hear the mantram in your dreams, reverberating in the depths of your consciousness. It is an exceedingly rewarding experience, and one which will protect you in your sleep. A friend once told me that he had long been subject to a certain recurrent nightmare, but one night, just as this nightmare was working up to its usual fearful climax, he heard the mantram echoing in his consciousness. It dispelled the fear and the bad dream, too, and that nightmare has never been back to haunt him again. So when you have learned to fall asleep in the mantram, it is goodbye to nightmares, to disquieting dreams, to that feeling that the night hasn't exactly been refreshing.

As you are learning to fall asleep in the mantram,

you are likely to be paying more attention than before to the process of falling asleep, and you may observe things which you have never noticed before. The body may give a sudden twitch, or you may hear little voices or even see things. There is nothing occult about this, and nothing to be alarmed at. If such experiences occur while you are falling asleep, pay no attention to them; just hang on to the mantram. Scientists call this twilight zone between waking and sleeping the hypnogogic state; I like to call it Alice's Wonderland. Before we are actually asleep, the conscious mind is closing up shop and the trap door to the subconscious may open a crack to let a few stray wisps of consciousness waft out. Pay no attention to them. They are not angelic voices and they are not clues to the innermost workings of your mind; they have no more significance than the everchanging shapes you can see in clouds drifting by. Quite possibly this sort of thing has always happened as you fell asleep, only you were not aware enough to notice. So when you are making an effort to fall asleep in the mantram, just go on repeating it if these wisps of consciousness come your way.

Falling asleep in the mantram is not as easy as it sounds. It takes some practice, but it is well worth the effort. So if you take a nap during the day, or doze off while riding in a car or bus or plane, or wake up in the middle of the night, just treat these events as opportunities for learning to fall asleep in the mantram. This is especially helpful for those who are subject to bouts of sleeplessness. Instead of lying there watching the clock, getting anxious about how much sleep you're missing or how you will feel in the morning, repeat the mantram. Then instead of complaining, "I missed two hours and forty-three minutes of sleep last night," you can say, "I had two hours and forty-three minutes of uninterrupted time for the mantram." With this change of perspective, and with the mantram soothing your mind, you may soon find yourself a complete stranger to insomnia. And of course in the morning there is nothing like the mantram for beginning the day. When your alarm goes off, you don't have to pull the covers over your head and lie there groaning; the mantram will enable you to fling off your covers and face the challenges of the day with enthusiasm.

Parents of small children will find the mantram a perfect lullaby. This is especially the case with infants, who may need a lot of attention during the night—a lot of walking, a lot of rocking, a lot of physical contact, all of which may take up several hours of the night. On such occasions, the mantram will not only soothe your baby but also give you the patience you need to get through the night, and it is so restful on a deeper level of consciousness that it can make up a great deal for the sleep you lose. When you use the mantram in this way, you are planting it deep in your child's consciousness, which will be an invaluable service to him or her in later years. Mahatma Gandhi absorbed his mantram, *Rama,* in this way, at his nurse's knee, just as I came to love the *Hare Rama* mantram from hearing it on my Granny's lips when I was a young child.

When we repeat the mantram we are calling on the Lord, however we conceive of him. The mantram is really one of the best of prayers—one that we say not just when we get up or when we go to bed, but countless times throughout the day, and throughout the night as well. This prayer is not addressed to some extraterrestrial being swinging between Neptune and Pluto, but to our deepest Self, the Lord of Love, who dwells in the hearts of us all. When we repeat the mantram, we are not asking for anything in particular, like good health or solutions to our problems or richer personal relationships. We are simply asking to get closer to the Lord, who is the source of all strength and all joy and all love. But as Jesus tells us, "Seek ye first the kingdom of heaven, and all else shall be added unto you." When we ask simply to get closer to the Lord, we find at the same time that our health improves, our problems begin to be resolved, and all our relationships grow richer and more fulfilling.

Keeping the Mind
Steady ❦

A tremendous amount of our vital energy is squandered in the vacillations of the mind as it swings towards what it likes and away from what it doesn't like. Most of us are so conditioned to go after what we like and avoid what we dislike that we do not even realize how enormous this problem is. When we are caught up in likes and dislikes, in strong opinions and set habits, we cannot work at our best, and we cannot know real security either. We live at the mercy of external circumstances: if things go our way, we get elated; if things do not go our way, we get depressed. It is only the mature person—the man or woman who is not conditioned by compulsive likes and dislikes, habits and opinions—who is really free in life. Such people are truly spontaneous. They can see issues clearly rather than through the distorting medium of strong opinions, and they can respond to people as they are and not as they imagine them to be.

The mantram can be of great value in learning

to keep the mind even and steady, for it gives the mind something to hold on to, something to steady itself by. In the Hindu tradition, we often compare the mind to the trunk of an elephant—restless, inquisitive, and always straying. If you watch an elephant sometime, you will see how apt the comparison is. In our towns and villages, caparisoned elephants are often taken in religious processions through the streets to the temple. The streets are crooked and narrow, lined on either side with fruit stalls and vegetable stalls. Along comes the elephant with his restless trunk, and in one sinuous motion it grabs a whole bunch of bananas. You can almost see him asking, "What else do you expect me to do? Here is my trunk and there are the bananas." He just doesn't know what else to do with his trunk. He doesn't pause to peel the bananas, either, or to observe all the other niceties that Emily Post says should be observed in eating a banana. He takes the whole bunch, opens his cavernous mouth, and tosses the bananas in stalk and all. Then from the next stall he picks up a coconut and tosses it in after the bananas. There is a loud crack and the elephant moves on to the next stall. No threats or promises can make this restless trunk settle down. But the wise mahout, if he knows his elephant well, will just give that trunk a short bamboo stick to hold on to before the procession starts. Then the elephant will walk along proudly with his head up high, holding the bamboo stick in front of him like a drum major with a baton. He is not interested in bananas or coconuts any more; his trunk has something to hold on to. The mind is very much like this. Most of the time it has nothing to hold on to, but we can keep it from straying into all kinds of absurd situations if we just give it the mantram.

In my childhood, boys learning to ride an elephant always tried to get the seat near the rope around the elephant's neck. The elephant's back is broad and none too steady as he walks, so the rope is very reassuring. When the elephant spies a ripe jackfruit high in a tree and reaches up to pluck it, so that you feel like you're sitting on one of those slides on a playground, you have the rope to hang on to. When the elephant bends down for a drink of water and you find yourself almost doing a headstand, you have the rope to hang on to. In life, when you find your mind going up towards elation and what it likes or down towards depression and what it dislikes, when your habits are thwarted and your opinions are contradicted, the mantram is the rope. But it is not enough just to remember the mantram at such times, although this helps greatly. We must also be able to strengthen our will and train it to help us make the wise choices which in the long run will free our minds from these vacillations.

Detachment from likes and dislikes, habits and

opinions, is not a negative quality at all. It is an enormously strong, positive quality which is the key to successful living. Freedom from likes and dislikes does not mean that life is insipid for us, but that we are not driven compulsively by rigid ways of thinking. Even if we don't get what we want—or if we do get what we don't want—we can still function cheerfully and efficiently. Similarly, detachment from habits does not mean that we have no habits. Good habits can be very useful in life. But we should be able to change our habits gracefully, or drop them altogether when necessary, especially if we learn that they are harmful to us or not exactly endearing to those around us. If we are used to a cup of coffee every morning with our breakfast and we come in one morning and discover that we're out of coffee, we don't say "I can't function without my coffee" and go back to bed; we should be able to say cheerfully, "I'll have tea, then."

It is much the same story with detachment from our opinions. Detachment from opinions does not mean that we are wishy-washy, that we do not have strong opinions on basic issues. It means that we have the forbearance not to force our opinions on others, and the security and strength of conviction not to get rattled when people question or contradict us. We should be able to make all sorts of graceful concessions on things that do not matter much in life and yet stand unshakable on essentials. Mahatma Gandhi, for example, was not in favor of tea or coffee, but he took joy in making a cup of tea for his wife each morning just the way she liked it. This is bending gracefully on nonessentials. When it came to essentials, however, Gandhi was unshakable. His dedication to nonviolence in word and deed was so absolute that he would abruptly call off a successful nationwide program of noncooperation with the British if he heard any reports of violence perpetrated by his countrymen, even those who did not acknowledge him as their leader.

So when I talk about strengthening the will, I mean cultivating detachment from likes and dislikes, habits and opinions, so that we may go against them if it is for the welfare of those around us. Self-will, self-centered behavior, is just the opposite: we cling obsessively to our likes and dislikes, to compulsive habits and opinions, and try to impose them on anyone who comes within our range. Reducing self-will has nothing to do with lack of will; on the contrary, our will grows stronger and stronger as we reduce our self-will.

Nothing in life is more satisfying, more masterful, than to be able to change our likes and dislikes when we need to. In fact, anyone who has mastered this skill has mastered life, and anyone who has not learned to overcome likes and dislikes is a victim of life. The statement we hear so often these days—"I like it, so I'm going to do it"—is a confession that that person is not free. When I say, "I am going to do this because I like it; I am not going to do that because I don't like it," what I am really saying is, "My hands are bound; I have no choice in life." This is our conditioning; we have always been encouraged to do the things we like doing, to do the things we are good at doing, and not encouraged to do the things we dislike. Our nervous system has become conditioned to one-way traffic, automatically flowing toward what we like and away from what we dislike. This is very much like trying to drive a car in which the steering wheel will turn only in one direction—say, only to the left. Even the simplest maneuver, like driving to the store, would be difficult. A car like this is not only a hindrance; it is very likely to end up in a crash. When you learn to go beyond your likes and dislikes, you are freeing the wheel to turn in both directions. This is a skill which everyone can learn through repetition of the mantram and exercising the will.

Just see what happens when circumstances force us to go against our likes and dislikes! If we have to do some job we dislike, even if it is for the welfare of all those around us, we get weak in the knees, our back begins to ache, we feel tired all over, and our will lies down and goes to sleep on the job. We make an appointment with the doctor to see if we have anemia or mononucleosis. And if we have to work with someone we don't like, we get irritated and frustrated; eventually we get all sorts of psychosomatic ailments, and finally we have to pack up and leave town. Moving away is how we naturally try to solve such problems, and I suppose later on, when interplanetary travel is commonplace, there will be people who give as their reason for leaving this earth, "I can't get far enough away from that person." But there is a magnificent alternative: instead of getting irritated with that person, you can be inspired to help him; instead of hating that person, you can come to love her. This is real mastery.

The person with strong likes and dislikes will try to move away from what he does not like doing and throw himself with extravagant zeal into what he does like doing. We have a pungent story from my old state of Kerala illustrating this. Here is a farmer at harvest time, looking at the fields of rice that must be cut, bundled, brought home, threshed, and stored. His livelihood depends on this. But it is a huge undertaking, and his will turns to jelly at the very thought of it. Then his eye falls on his bullock cart, and he notices how dilapidated it has come to look. In a flash of inspiration, he decides to paint it. The project fires him with enthusiasm. He doesn't just go to a paint store and buy a can of off-white enamel; he plans the design painstakingly, finds his own natural pigments, and mixes just the right colors with elaborate care. And then, while the rice stands in the fields still waiting to be harvested, he settles down to paint intricate floral designs on the cartwheel.

We are all adept at painting bullock cart wheels. When our term paper is three weeks late, we decide it is time to take apart our motorcycle. When it is time to sit down and write thank-you notes, we have an irresistible urge to reorganize our closet. When it is time to get back to work on our income tax report, we pick up a six-month-old magazine and read an article on dinosaurs with avid interest. I am not too much impressed by a person who works hard at a job he likes; what really wins my admiration is when a person is able to do a job he dislikes with cheerfulness and zest if it benefits those around him.

Overcoming Rigidity

People who have strong likes and dislikes find life very difficult; they are as rigid as if they had only one bone. Such people cannot bend, and if they are compelled to bend, they can only break. There is only one position they can take—absolute rigidity. Today this rigidity begins to set in very early in life. In my university days, when my students would call some white-haired member of the faculty an old fogey, I used to tell them that fogeyishness is not confined to any particular age group. There *are* old people who are old fogeys, but I have also seen young fogeys, too. The fogey is anyone who cannot change his opinions, who cannot see beyond her likes and dislikes, who is locked into old habits and cannot yield gracefully.

None of us has to become an old fogey just because we are growing older. But the capacity to be flexible naturally, to change likes and dislikes without much resistance, comes especially easily to the young, and we are not doing our children any favor when we undermine this capacity by always catering to their likes and dislikes. If I may be blunt, we are crippling them for life. As usual, my Grandmother understood this very well. When I was a boy, she would sometimes say to me as I was leaving for school in the morning, "Son, why don't you sit next to someone you don't like today?" The very thought used to make my skin crawl, but because I loved her very much, I would dutifully go and sit down next to some other little boy of whom I was not particularly fond. At first I would be keenly aware of who was sitting by my side. Part of my attention would be on the teacher and part on this boy whom I didn't exactly like. But as I became absorbed in what the teacher was saying, whether it was about geography or English or history, I found that I forgot all about who was sitting next to me—and oddly enough, as soon as I discovered that I didn't mind sitting next to him, I realized that I didn't really dislike him after all. In the meantime, of course, he was deciding the very same thing about me. It is in little ways like this that my Granny taught me how to change my likes and dislikes at will.

Rigidity creeps up on us, and it can come very early in life. I had a friend like that even as a university student; when we would go to a restaurant, he would sit down and immediately begin to rearrange the plate, the silverware, the napkin, the glass, the chair—everything. He had a particular kind of eating arrangement which he had to work out everywhere he went. For such people there is a very apt phrase in my mother tongue. When a student isn't doing his arithmetic very well, for example, and the teacher asks why, the student replies, "I don't know; I can do it just fine under my mango tree." In other words, he is saying "I require a particular set of conditions, and if you take me away from my mango tree, I can't even count to ten." Such a person depends for his security on external circumstances, and when we go through life having to have everything just right before we can function, we will find it difficult to adjust, to be resilient.

But we can all learn to develop resilience. We

can make ourselves like that Japanese doll called the daruma doll, which has a rounded base and is weighted in such a way that when you push it over, it springs back up. You can hold it down as long as you like, but as soon as you take your hand away, it jumps back up again. This is the kind of resilience that we can all culti-vate. Whenever life tries to knock down people who have developed this precious quality of resilience, they are able to spring back; they have lost every trace of rigidity.

When we let rigidity and inflexibility set in, it is a sign that we are losing our vitality, too. When you find a difficult situation at home or at work or in personal relationships and you run away from that situation, you are saying, "I am made of one bone; I can only take one position." This is rigor mortis. It is dying not to be able to yield; it is dying not to be able to bend.

There is a strong story from the Indian tradition which shows what happens to people who cannot bend. As the Ganges river flows down from the Hima-layas, it uproots big trees and carries them down into the plains. A sage noticed this and asked the river, "How is it that you tear out these huge pine trees and yet leave the willow and the reed and the tall grasses that grow by your banks?" The Ganges replied, "The pine tree doesn't know how to bend; it stands rigid

103

and won't move out of my way, so I pull it out by the root and take it with me down to the sea. But these willows and reeds and grasses bend when I come; they do not resist me. I sing through them, and I leave them intact."

Once rigidity has set in, we are unable to change our likes and dislikes or our opinions, no matter how disastrous it may be to go on clinging to them. For example, even though salt is known to aggravate high blood pressure, many people suffering from this condition would rather take a potent drug than reduce the amount of salt in their diet, just because they have come to like highly seasoned, highly spiced food. In fact, I have heard that doctors often do not even recommend to such patients that they reduce their salt intake, because they will not only fail to heed this advice but are likely to start ignoring some of the doctor's other directions as well. But I am not criticizing such people; it is extremely difficult to change our likes and dislikes without some mastery over the thinking process. It is this kind of mastery which we cultivate by repeating the mantram and learning to exercise our will.

But let me tell you a story—also about salt—which shows what artistry there is in dropping old likes and dislikes without a backward glance, and what a strong influence our personal example can be. When I was a boy, my village doctor once put me on a salt-free diet for a year. In a tropical climate like India's, salt is very important, and it is almost impossible for most Indians to imagine food without salt or spices. So I bewailed my fate loudly. I didn't get much help from my friends at school: "No salt for a year? You might as well quit eating." My mother didn't know what to tell me either; all she could say was that it was only for one year, which didn't exactly console me. I just didn't know how I was going to get through three hundred and sixty-five days with no salt. But the next morning, as I sat down dejectedly to my first saltless breakfast, my Grandmother seated herself by my side and said quietly, "I have gone off salt for a year too." And she didn't merely tolerate that saltless food; she ate it with real gusto, because she knew that her example was supporting me. As for me, I don't think I ever tasted a better meal than that saltless breakfast my Grandmother shared with me. In one simple gesture, she showed her love with innate artistry. We can all learn to change our likes and dislikes like this when necessary, particularly when it is in the best interests of others, and with this capacity there comes a great sense of freedom.

Freedom in Personal Relationships

People with strong likes and dislikes are often extremely self-centered; they often have fierce self-will. Sooner or later this self-will is going to be violated, because sooner or later the person with strong likes and dislikes will gravitate toward another person with equally strong likes and dislikes who will contradict him. I have seen many partnerships which have been formed in just this way, especially between men and women. If one party contradicts, the other will contradict with compound interest, and the children of such people grow up handicapped for life. So when people with fierce likes and dislikes are contradicted, when they find themselves in situations where their self-will is violated—which is absolutely inevitable—a host of disastrous consequences ensue. Personal relationships deteriorate, emotional security vanishes, there is constant mental turmoil, and all sorts of psychosomatic problems arise: breathing problems, digestive problems, allergies, and even cardiovascular problems. So you can see that freeing ourselves from the tyranny of likes and dislikes is not just of theoretical importance. It can solve emotional problems and often physical problems as well, and it never fails to make for richer personal relationships.

This last point is of utmost importance in our modern age, which often seems to me to be the age of loneliness. Being able to go beyond your own likes and dislikes helps immensely in restoring the personal relationships that make life worth living, for it enables us to be patient, cheerful, and loving with those around us. A good deal of our agitation in personal relationships stems from the inevitable fact that others do not always share our opinions, our likes and dislikes. What we are really saying in such cases is, "Why don't you behave the way *I* think you should behave? Why don't you think the way *I* think you should think? Don't you realize how much you are upsetting me?"

Ultimately we have only two ways out of this dilemma. Either we can work hard to get others to behave as we would like them to behave—which is likely to be a rather long pull—or we can work to change our own responses to others. Most of us seem to have decided that it is easier to try to get others to change. We want others to dress as we would like them to dress, to speak and act as we would like them to speak and act, to change all the innumerable little habits which we find so annoying—the way he clears his throat, the way she laughs, the way so-and-so stirs his tea. This is a full-time job, since you will have to work on not just one person but on everyone you come in contact with; and the more entrenched your likes and dislikes are, the more miraculous is the transformation you expect all these people to make. But consider the alternative. Wouldn't it take far less time and far less energy, and be far more rewarding too, if we could learn to change our responses to others? When we begin to free ourselves from likes and dislikes, this is just what we are learning to do—to change our responses not just to our partner or our children or our parents, but to anyone.

A good deal of the friction in personal relationships stems from our inability to respect the ways and the opinions of others. Very often when people come to me and announce that they have moved out of their parents' home, left their boyfriend or girlfriend, or terminated an old friendship, they explain by saying, "We had irreconcilably different philosophies of life." If I may be blunt, the problem is not irreconcilable differences in philosophy, as if you and your estranged partner used to debate free will versus predestination; it is simply that neither was flexible enough to concede that the other has a valid point of view.

When you are capable of juggling with your likes and dislikes, there is no turmoil. No one can offend your self-will because you will have very little of it. If someone is angry, you can be detached and look at the issue from that person's point of view; if someone is attacking you, you can listen attentively and see if there isn't something in what they say. Your very attitude of forbearance and sympathy will enable the other person also to make a greater effort to understand your point of view.

In my university days in India, I once had a colleague who irritated me in every way. Not only were his mannerisms annoying, but he also had an uncanny knack of contradicting my pet opinions. I didn't even have to be with him to be irritated; even in a conversation with someone else he would raise his voice loud enough to make sure I overheard as he made a few opprobrious remarks about my favorite authors. I used to make a point of keeping as far as possible from this man. But when I came to realize the mastery that comes with going beyond likes and dislikes, I began to look upon encounters with him as opportunities. One day, when he was holding forth on some subject or other at which we had always been at loggerheads, I repeated the mantram with greater determination than ever, went over to his chair, and sat down right next to him. He could scarcely believe his eyes. "Let me hear what you have to say," I said—and not as a challenge, either, but with genuine interest. We talked for a while, and I listened carefully to every word he said. To my surprise, I found that he really didn't agitate me after all. He had been contradicting some of my favorite opinions, but when I was no longer obsessively identified with these opinions, my security was in no way shaken. Not only that, my example of detachment helped him, too, for after we had been talking for a while, he told me, "You know, there might be something in what you say." I must admit that I too began to see something in his point of view.

There is no more perfect context for learning to reduce likes and dislikes than the relationship between man and woman. Our usual notions of romance—sending flowers, dining in candle-lit restaurants so dim that we need a flashlight to read the menu—these things are just games. Real romance lies in learning to take joy in what our partner likes, in learning to change our habits and opinions to accommodate those of our partner and to think of our partner's needs before our own. This is very difficult, but it is the essence of a romance which will never fade, never cloy, but only grow deeper and richer with the passage of time.

Freeing ourselves from compulsive likes and dislikes is essential for cooperation anywhere, whether in the home or in the office, and cooperation is the perfect antidote to deteriorating relationships. Competition, on the other hand, can only divide us. Competition is debilitating wherever we find it in life, and nowhere is it more disastrous than in the home, between man and woman. I am entirely in sympathy with women's protests that they have been exploited and taken for granted by men, but when women try to compete with men, when they retaliate and become aggressive, they are copying what is least admirable in men. They are weakening themselves, and they are weakening the men around them too. When the mother and father make the home into a battleground, it cripples the children for life; they will grow up with a division in their consciousness which very few will ever be able to heal. If one person will only take the first step—and, if necessary, the second, and the third—in trying to communicate and to see the other's point of view, there are very few disagreements that cannot be resolved in a way that brings both people closer together. Gandhi tells us with characteristic candor that the stormy scenes of his early married life ceased when he quit insisting that his wife respect his rights and began paying more attention to his responsibilities instead. We are not here to compete with one another; we have come into this world to complete one another, and this is especially true of husband and wife.

I come from a matrilineal tradition in Kerala, where I had the inestimable privilege of growing up surrounded by women who were the embodiment of gentleness, patience, and self-forgetfulness. This is real strength, and it comes naturally to women. Far from trying to exploit these qualities or take them for granted, the men in my ancestral family were transformed by the personal example of the women around them. The woman who holds together a home in which her menfolk and the children can absorb these price-less qualities is making a great contribution to life, and she is fulfilling herself and those around her far more than if she learns to drive a truck or brings home a larger paycheck than her husband. When I say this, sometimes people ask, "Are you saying that woman's place is in the home then?" I reply, "Yes, and *man's* place is in the home too." There need be no conflict between one's profession and one's family, but for both men and women—especially in these days when family unity has been all but forgotten—it is the family that must come first.

Competition is in the very air today, on the international scene as well as in the office, on the campus, and in the home. Comparing ourselves with others, envying others, only aggravates competition. What we forget when we envy others is that every job, every position, every role has some element of drudgery, some unpleasant aspect or heavy responsibility. Writing, for example, is a job which we often hear glamorized as being creative and artistic, but according to one writer's confession, it is one percent inspiration and ninety-nine percent perspiration. We think of the writer with pen poised, waiting for the muse to speak, and we forget that he often has to spend hours with a red pencil polishing up what the muse has told him—when she bothers to speak to him at all. The way we should evaluate a job is not to ask what we like about it or dislike about it, whether it pays better than our partner's or is more prestigious; what we should ask is, does it contribute to the welfare of others? If it does, it is a good job, and there is no need to compare it to what others do. But if it is at the cost of life or of the welfare of others, we should turn our backs on it; it is not right occupation. In this sense, the person who shines shoes for a living is a much more beneficial member of society than the person who manufactures cigarettes.

When we are tempted to compete and compare ourselves with others, we should remember that each of us has some special capacity. If you do not have the same capacity as someone else, that is no cause for envy or self-criticism; you have some other capacity. Just take physical capacities, for example. When I was watching the Olympics on television, I was amazed at some of the feats that the human being can accomplish through will, proper training, and making the most of his or her capacities. The Russian fellow who won the gold medal in weight lifting really impressed me; he was huge, about five times as broad as I am, and built like a bull. And then there was the winner of the pole vault, long and lean, built for hurling himself through the air. Just imagine the absurdity of it if instead of lifting weights, this mountain of a man had tried to catapult himself over the bar in the pole vault, or if the willowy pole-vaulter had tried to lift five hundred pounds!

Each of us is unique in his or her own way, and each has some special contribution to make to life around us. But I never tire of repeating that all these differences, which make life interesting, are only one percent; what unites us is the ninety-nine percent that we all have in common. As the Bible says, we are all made in the image of the Lord; we all have our root in the Divine Ground of existence. When we keep this underlying unity in mind, we can appreciate individual differences without any comparisons or implications of superiority or inferiority. But what most of us have been conditioned to do is to keep our eyes firmly fixed on the one percent, and when we see some difference between people we automatically assume that one is superior and the other inferior. We could save ourselves a good deal of wasted energy and needless agitation if we could unlearn the habit of comparing ourselves with others, and here, of course, the mantram can come to our rescue. If we can repeat the mantram when we find ourselves falling into competitiveness and invidious comparison, it will help greatly to keep our minds calm and our relationships secure.

Learning to Do What We Dislike

In addition to repetition of the mantram, there are a number of very simple, practical steps which you can take to free yourself from the clutches of likes and dislikes: doing cheerfully things you dislike, not postponing disagreeable tasks, and learning to drop at will work that you are caught up in. These are some of the basic skills of living in freedom.

To see why the repetition of the mantram can be so valuable in overcoming likes and dislikes, just try to watch your mind with a little detachment when you have an opportunity to do something you like or when circumstances force you to do something you dislike. In either case, the mind gets more and more out of control. When it is something you like—an unexpected day off, a chance to go to your favorite restaurant, some time to work on your pet project—the mind gets excited and begins to quiver with anticipation. "How wonderful! How marvelous!" When it is something you dislike—doing a job you detest, working with someone who rubs you the wrong way, having to go to an Italian restaurant when your heart is set on Chinese food—the mind begins to shiver with apprehension and kicks up a cloud of protests. "This isn't fair! Why should it happen to me? Maybe I can palm this one off on someone else." Any motion of the mind consumes some of our vital energy, and the storms raised by likes and dislikes consume a good deal of power. It is at times like these that the mantram is invaluable. You can conserve a tremendous amount of vital energy by repeating the mantram and not letting your mind go through these wild oscillations. This will be difficult at first, but the pendulum of the mind will swing less and less as you send the mantram deeper into your consciousness.

One of the best ways of freeing ourselves from compulsive likes and dislikes is to do things we dislike doing, especially if they are for the welfare of our family or friends. Then we should be able to say, "I'll go and do it, and I'll do it with a smile." When my Grandmother would tell me this, I was always very respectful, but I used to tell her honestly, "I'll do it, Granny, but not with a smile." The capacity to "do it with a smile" is a sign of real maturity, and personal example, especially with young people, is the very best way in which this capacity can be taught. This is the way we show our love, and it can be done in many ways. When you want to go to a show, instead of insisting that your family go to the show you like, go to the show they like. Just see how difficult it is. You have been dreaming about Elton John; you have all his albums, his photograph; you have saved the money and reserved the seat—all for Elton. You have been looking forward to his concert all week. Then, in the evening, you tell your family, "I am not going to the Elton John program; I am going to the opera that you all want to see." You see what daring this requires, what courage. Repeating the mantram will help you summon up the will to make this decision, and the mantram will give you the resolve to stick by it. And of course, whenever you are tempted to blurt out, "I'm really dying to see Elton John; I'm only going to the opera for your sake, even if it kills me," that is the time to keep repeating the mantram. And you don't go to the opera house and sit there like a wet blanket, either; you radiate joy. Afterwards, when the conductor comes up to congratulate you on being a born lover of opera, you can say, "Actually, I don't understand opera. But I love my family, and I take joy in their joy."

The way to tackle a job you dislike is by giving it more of your attention. This may sound very simple, but let me assure you that it is very effective. Now when we get a job we don't like, we protest that we are artists, that this job is drudgery and we require work which challenges our creative talents. Very often this is just a euphemistic way of saying that the job is one we don't like doing. If the job is one that really needs to be done, stifle your protests, repeat the mantram, and get to work. If we can just give more of our attention to work we dislike, we find that it becomes tolerable and even interesting. Giving our full attention works wonders with any task. Suppose you have to clear away some weeds in the backyard. Don't think about how hot it is, how tired you are, or how much you'd rather be at the pool; remind yourself that the weeds are unsightly, they are a fire hazard, and *someone* has to do the job. You don't just take a few listless whacks at the first weed and then wander off, either; instead, you get to work. You feel a real sense of accomplishment as the weeds fall, and soon you are seeking them out: "Aha, there's another one behind the steps!" Finally you get so absorbed that if someone brings out a glass of lemonade for you, you find yourself saying, "Thanks, but I can't stop now." By giving it your full attention, you have turned a job you formerly detested into work that you find rewarding, and you have strengthened your will in the bargain.

It is sometimes helpful to remember that our likes and dislikes, our tastes and our opinions, however rigid they may seem now, were not always this way. Very often we have worked hard to acquire a particular like, to cultivate a particular taste. Let me take just one example which must be familiar to all of you: beer. In my university days in India, as a professor of English literature, I used to read in many plays and novels about the glories of beer—what a marvelous beverage it is, what conviviality it evokes. And so one day a friend and I decided that we would have to try this beer for ourselves. We went to a place frequented by the British, sat down nonchalantly like men of the world, and placed our order. The waiter brought us a big bottle, opened it for us with a flourish, and stood back to enjoy the show. We never knew there was any special art to pouring beer, so when we poured it, it foamed and foamed. In a few seconds the glass was full of foam and there was only a little liquid at the bottom. When we finally managed to get the beer to our lips through all that foam, we just couldn't believe how bitter it was. We couldn't take more than a few swallows of the stuff. This was the drink whose praises I heard sung so lavishly! Now I have tremendous respect for anyone who can control his palate enough to learn not only to drink beer but to enjoy it, too. Anyone who has put that much effort into acquiring a taste should certainly be able to put that same effort into setting himself free from the tyranny of likes and dislikes too.

Gradually, with the help of the mantram, you learn to change your old responses, and once you get the secret of it, this can be done everywhere you go. You learn to refrain from doing things you like, cheerfully and without complaint, if that will benefit those around you. You learn to do things you dislike with real enthusiasm and zest, if they are for the welfare of

119

others. You are beginning to enjoy things that you formerly disliked, and of course you still enjoy the things you like. So you have lost nothing; you have gained. You are able to enjoy more in life and you have made yourself freer, too.

Not Postponing Jobs We Dislike

Another way to free ourselves from likes and dislikes is not to put off the jobs we dislike. Most of us have been conditioned to do the jobs we like first; we leave the disagreeable job for last. My Grandmother sometimes used to ask me to do something important, but I had so many unimportant things of my own to attend to that the task she had entrusted to me didn't always get done. When she would ask, "When are you going to do it?" I would answer, "One of these days, Granny." She wasn't impressed. "One of these days is none of these days." When you hear someone say, "I'm going to get around to it one of these days," you can be sure that it isn't going to get done. The mark of the mature person is the capacity to take up a job immediately— "forthwith," as Jesus says—and do it cheerfully and with concentration.

When we postpone a disagreeable job, we may be hoping that someone else will do it for us if we wait long enough. This is not too likely. Swami Ramdas, one of the most delightful saints of modern India, has a story about people who try to get others to do their work for them. There was a field of rice in which a family of sparrows had its nest, and when harvest time came, the man who owned the field called his friend and said, "When you have time, please harvest this rice." The little sparrows heard this and they flew back to the father sparrow and said, "Our home is going to be destroyed." The father sparrow asked, "Where did you hear this?" "We heard the owner of the field telling his friend." The father sparrow knew a good deal about the ways of human beings, and he asked, "What exactly did he say?" "He said, 'When you have time, please harvest this rice.'" Father sparrow laughed. "Don't worry," he assured his little ones, "we have nothing to fear."

Days went by and the field still hadn't been harvested. The owner of the field called his son, who had many irons in the fire and led a rather active night life, and told him, "My friend doesn't seem too enthusiastic about this harvest, so I would like you to harvest the rice." The young man said, "All right, dad, when I feel equal to it." The little sparrows heard this too, so they flew back to father sparrow and told him, "This time the owner's son is going to harvest the field." "What exactly did he say?" "He said, 'When I feel equal to it.'" Father sparrow laughed again and told them not to worry. The owner's son had his night life, he had his day life, he had his hundred and one irons in the fire, and he never did feel equal to harvesting the rice.

Finally, one day, the owner got up and said, "I'm going to harvest the field myself." The little sparrows heard this, too. Acting on precedent, they came and told their father, "We know there's no need to worry, father, but we just heard the owner saying that he is going to harvest the field himself." Father sparrow dropped everything and jumped to his feet. "Quick! Pack everything and let's get out! He's going to do it himself; that means it is going to get done."

When we postpone a disagreeable job, we may be wishing that it would miraculously vanish if we ignored it long enough. But jobs we put off have a way of not vanishing, and in fact, they have a way of getting more difficult with the passage of time. In this connection, my Grandmother used to say, "He who postpones will have to carry a mountain on his back." Months ago that loose hinge on the screen door would have taken only a few minutes to fix; now the other hinge has worked loose and the door has fallen off in the wind, and torn the screen as well. We could have started our term paper weeks ago and worked on it steadily all along, but now there's just three days left, not only to write our term paper but to study for the final and read all the books for the course too. When we postpone things in this way, things pile up and we end up carrying a mountain of work which we could have avoided very easily.

So when you have a job you dislike, instead of putting it off, put it at the very top of your list of priorities. And don't dawdle over it; do it with real enthusiasm. Then there will still be time for the jobs you like, and you will find them more enjoyable when you are that much freer. You won't be doing them under the cloud of dreading the disagreeable job, you won't be doing them under compulsion, and you will have made your will a little stronger.

How do we begin a job that we have been putting off, especially one that we have been dreading? People have often asked me for some simple secret. "It is so overwhelming that we just don't know where to start," they say. "Where do we begin?" A frontal assault is very difficult; even with the best of intentions, we often can't just sit down and start composing the opening paragraph of our long-overdue term paper. But there is a simple trick that works. Repeat the mantram a few times and take a deep breath; then clear off your desk, sharpen your pencil, pull out the books you need, and spread out your notes *as if* you were going to get to work. When your mind complains, "I just can't face it," reassure it that you are just going to leaf through the books, sort the notes, and push the pencil around a little. Then, to play fair and keep your mind at ease, you do just that: leaf through the books a little, sort your notes, jot down a stray idea that occurs to you— it doesn't really much matter what. Soon, despite your lack of intentions, there is another stray idea; then, as you skim a page, a couple of ideas fall into place, and you read a little further and get a few more ideas and write down some new insights. Before you know it, you have gotten absorbed in the project: there is enthusiasm, there is a steady flow of ideas, and you are working with real concentration. You must have noticed how step by step you can get embroiled in little jobs you hadn't set out to do; here, you are putting that same tendency to work for you instead of letting it work against you. This is the way to get the job done; it helps concentration, it strengthens the will.

Learning to Drop a Job at Will

It is good to be enthusiastic in the struggle against the tyranny of likes and dislikes, but it is also important to use your discrimination too. It is not really very helpful to say, "I love home-baked bread, so I will give it up; I will never eat home-baked bread again." It is much more artistic—and much more sensible, too—to go on eating home-baked bread, but in moderation. As long as they are not at the expense of ourselves or anyone else, there is no harm in doing the things we like, *provided* we can do them in freedom. In practical terms, this means that we can do these things in moderation and that we are able to drop them at will.

This ability to drop something we like at will is a very important step in freeing ourselves from likes and dislikes. When we are doing a job we dislike, we can drop it on the slightest pretext without a second thought. But just see how difficult this is when we are compulsively caught up in something! When we are reading our favorite author or working on our pet project and something comes up which demands more urgent attention, it is very difficult for the mind to drop what it is absorbed in. And in the evening, when we leave our office or our campus, our work comes running after us, yapping like a little terrier at our heels. We don't really taste our dinner, we don't really hear what our family and friends are saying to us, we don't really perceive the needs of others, all because this little terrier keeps yapping in the back of our minds. It is good to work hard and apply ourselves completely to our work, but we should never let ourselves be driven by it.

All too often, once we have let ourselves get obsessed with some job—say, writing a report the boss has asked for at work—we aren't able to get the thought of it out of our minds. While we are showering we find ourselves composing clever topic sentences; while walking along the street we find ourselves thinking of an apt statistic to work in; while falling asleep we see a better way to organize everything. These are all excellent times to repeat the mantram. You will be freeing yourself from the constant burden of your project, and you will find that repeating the mantram at such times actually improves your performance when you are able to get back to work again.

Learning to drop work at a moment's notice is one of the great spiritual disciplines practiced in Catholic convents and monasteries. Saint Theresa of Lisieux tells us that when the bell for prayer rang, she trained herself to put down her sewing without even finishing the stitch she was on. Imagine the patience and effort required to master this art of dropping work without so much as a ripple of protest in the mind! Most of us, when we are caught in something we like and we hear the call for dinner, say, "Oh, all right; just let me finish the page I'm reading." And we probably read a few pages more in the bargain.

This skill of learning to drop work at will has many practical consequences. In his late seventies, Mahatma Gandhi was able to do ten times the work of most men half his age. Everything he did, everything he wrote, carried immense responsibility because the major part of a vast nation trusted him completely. Yet he carried these responsibilities fifteen hours a day, seven days a week, without tension and fatigue, because he was able to drop his work at will. When a matter came to his attention, he would give it his complete concentration—concentration so intense that it pierced to the heart of any problem. Then he was able to set it aside and give all his concentration to the next problem without any distraction over the first.

When we haven't learned to drop our work at will like this, our concentration suffers, our work suffers, and even our personal relationships suffer. When we have turned over in our mind the possible solutions to a problem for the fiftieth time, the fifty-first time is not likely to be any more productive. In fact, it only consumes more of our vital energy as the mind runs on and on out of control. This is the time to remember the mantram. If we can just quit worrying about all the possible solutions, which the mantram can help us to do, we will often find that a better solution than any we had yet thought of will pop up from a deeper level of consciousness—perhaps even as we are saying the mantram.

In this connection, let me share with you a simple secret about memory. If you find yourself unable to recall some fact, some name, some line of poetry, don't stop and grit your teeth trying to remember it; this will only disrupt your train of thought. Just drop your attachment to remembering it, repeat the mantram a

127

couple of times, and proceed without it, unconcerned. Soon the fact, the name, the line of poetry will be tugging at your sleeve saying, "Here I am—'William the Conqueror, 1066.'"

Even worse than not being able to drop our work, but closely related to it, is not being able to drop our personal problems. Emotional problems particularly can haunt us wherever we go. There is a story that Mark Twain was asked by someone if he wouldn't like to go off on a vacation somewhere. "I'd be glad to," Twain replied, "if only I didn't have to take that fellow Mark Twain with me." When we drag personal problems about with us, dwelling on them, thinking about them, talking about them, even writing sonnets about them, life becomes a burden for us. If we could solve personal problems by thinking about them all the time, I would be all for it; if it resolved emotional conflicts to keep talking about them, I would say talk, talk, talk. But an intellectual understanding of our problems cannot give us the will or the wisdom to resolve them, and constantly dwelling on such problems only increases our identification with them. As the Buddha asks very penetratingly, how can we solve the problems of life with the mind, which is itself a problem? So when you find yourself caught in personal problems, that is the time to repeat the mantram and try to think more of the needs of those around you. When you are able to look at them more objectively, problems which once looked insurmountable will shrink to a manageable size.

As we begin to practice this skill, we will be surprised to see how often our self-will expresses itself in rigid opinions over the simplest things—having to have the seat by the aisle, for example, or not being able to drink our coffee unless it is at exactly one hundred and sixty degrees. Little habits like these can be sources of irritation when we have to deal with people who do not do things our way, and because they are such small habits, we can practice juggling with them easily. In this way we can learn to take on even our biggest likes and dislikes, especially those which hamper our relations with those around us. This is where real freedom lies. It is quite an accomplishment to be able to work harmoniously with people whose ways are not our ways and to relate cheerfully to those who irritate us. If we can learn to do this, we shall not only be benefiting ourselves, but through our personal example we shall be benefiting all those who come in contact with us, too.

The ability to work on a job with complete concentration and then put it completely out of your mind when necessary is a skill which we can all cultivate. Once you begin looking, you will find that every day is full of opportunities. Of course, it is important to keep a sense of discrimination too. If you are working on your income tax form, which must be postmarked by midnight that night, and someone suggests going to a movie, you don't jump up and say, "Yes, I'll go; I have to prove I'm not tied to my income tax form." But especially when it benefits someone around you, it is good to drop what you are doing and give your attention to what is most important to them. When you are absorbed in a favorite book and your partner interrupts you, you can set the book aside and give your complete attention to what they are saying. You can try to tell any nagging thought about the book: "Not now; I'm busy. I'll pay attention to you after this conversation is done." There should be no division in the mind, part of it on your conversation and part on what you have been reading. Division only makes for tension; complete concentration is complete relaxation. And when you find your mind persistently dogged by thoughts of your work, your project, your plans—especially at night, when you can't sleep—repeating the mantram can help you drop these nagging thoughts completely. This is a skill that will help your concentration, improve your peace of mind, help you to free yourself from compulsive likes and dislikes, and contribute greatly to strengthening your will—and it is a skill which everyone can develop through the help of the mantram and persistent practice.

Elation & Depression ❧

Elation and depression are words we hear constantly these days. When we meet someone, it is a safe bet that he or she is just going into a depression, or is in the middle of a depression, or is just coming out of a depression. We have come to look upon this as inevitable. On the other hand, we cultivate excitement everywhere—exciting vacations to the Bahamas, exciting new career possibilities, even exciting breakfast cereals. We are constantly conditioned to seek excitement; we are brainwashed to believe that we are not getting anything out of life unless we are excited. Yet it is one of the laws of nature that what goes up must come down, so we should not be surprised that depression has now reached epidemic proportions.

In my vocabulary, elation and depression go together as naturally as hot and cold or Dr. Jekyll and Mr. Hyde. They are Siamese twins, and we cannot court one without courting the other too. When we let ourselves get carried away by elation, we are opening the door for depression to visit us soon after. Whether we are elated or depressed, the mind is spinning out of our control, and the only difference is whether it is spinning over what is pleasant or what is unpleasant. The depressed person may look passive, but his mind is just as active and agitated as that of the excited person who is running around gesticulating and speaking wildly. When the mind is agitated, attention is scattered and concentration is difficult; so the person who is prone to elation and depression will find it hard to be effective at work, steadfast in personal relationships, and secure within.

Most people have little objection to getting elated, but none of us are very eager to see depression setting in. We don't mind being told not to get depressed, but "Don't let yourself get elated" may have a puritanical ring to it. Steering a middle course between elation and depression is not resigning ourselves to a flat and monotonous life—far from it. There is a third state which is neither elation nor depression, and if we can go beyond these two extremes, we will find the abiding joy which is our real nature.

When you are able to see the specter of depression lurking behind elation and have some personal experience of the joy which transcends both, you will come to look upon excitement with profound suspicion. I remember once seeing the picture of the winner of a beauty contest, taken at the instant she heard that she had won. At the risk of seeming unchivalrous, I must say that the sight of her features contorted in excitement was anything but beautiful. We see the mature reaction to success in a wise statement attributed to the late President Kennedy. On the day of his inauguration, a reporter asked him, "Mr. President, aren't you very excited on this great occasion?" Kennedy replied, "No, not excited—very interested."

People abandon themselves to elation in different ways. Some begin to talk and talk. Their ship has come home, their horse has won, their article has been accepted for publication, and they have to let everybody know. They pick up the telephone and call people they haven't seen in six months to tell them the good news, not because they are interested in what the other person has to say but because they must find an opportunity to express their excitement. Other people begin to find everything inordinately funny, and at the slightest provocation they will laugh until they can scarcely catch their breath. Wholesome laughter is a welcome relaxation, when it is not at anyone else's expense, but the wild laughter of excitement only leaves us prone to irritability later on.

Some people make elaborate plans or have grandiose visions of the future. If they have written a poem and someone praises it, it is only a matter of time before they envision their book of verse going into its tenth printing and crowds of admirers fighting to get their autograph; next they are composing their acceptance speech for the Nobel prize. Perhaps saddest of all, there are people who respond to elation with a flood of self-confidence, with plans and dreams far beyond their capacity to realize. They drive themselves to work harder and harder; they can't bear to hear their opinions contradicted or their plans and ambitions questioned; yet a short time later, when depression has struck, they will be doubting everything they do.

Whatever form elation takes, it is only agitation, a storm in the mind which we have been conditioned to regard as pleasant. When the mind oscillates wildly over good news, over pleasant prospects and unlimited possibilities, all this means is that we are dwelling more on ourselves and less on the needs of those around us. And once we have set the pendulum of the mind swinging, the inevitable reaction has to set in sooner or later. When that happens, we will still be dwelling on ourselves, but only on what is negative: the bad news, the unpleasant prospects, how ineffectual we are. I used to see this often in my university days, when I was in charge of the debating society. When we won a debate, some of the students would get so excited that their bodies would be trembling and they wouldn't be able to speak coherently. The next day they would be sleeping in class, and when I would rouse them to ask why they weren't able to keep awake, they would reply, "I couldn't get to sleep last night." Some of the brighter students would make the connection and add, "Maybe our winning the debate wasn't so good after all." "No," I used to answer, "winning the debate was fine. It was your reaction to it which made it impossible for you to sleep."

In medical circles there is a tendency to look upon depression as something from which none of us can escape, and a good deal of research is going into how to cure it. But depression is not physical; depression is in the mind. It is possible to relieve the symptoms, but we will never be able to set right the cause of depression through change of diet or powerful drugs or even surgery. A few extreme cases may call for such drastic measures, but it is my submission that most people could banish depression from their lives by observing a few simple rules of right living. When we resort instead to powerful mood-changing drugs, we are actually crippling ourselves. It *is* easier to take a pill than to change our pattern of living, but in suppressing depression through drugs or surgery, we are actually suppressing our capacity for creativity, for sensitivity to others, for drawing on our own deeper resources to go beyond elation and depression to a state of permanent joy. Depression is not inevitable;

it is a luxury which we buy at great cost to ourselves and to those around us.

Guarding Against Depression

All of us can guard ourselves against depression by taking a few simple steps. The most effective of these steps is not to let ourselves get excited or elated, and the best way to accomplish this is to work at overcoming likes and dislikes and to repeat the mantram. Whenever we work at reducing the tyranny of likes and dislikes, of habits and opinions, we are helping to safeguard ourselves against depression. Then, whether we win the Irish sweepstakes or our horse finishes last, the pendulum of the mind will not be set in motion. Whether things go our way or someone else's, we can always repeat the mantram and remain calm.

It is important to do this whenever things are going against us, but it is even more important when things are going *for* us, when excitement is rising and everything looks wonderful. In other words, do not wait for depression to come knocking at the door. It is difficult to remember to stay calm and repeat the mantram in the face of excitement, I admit, but it is far more difficult once depression has set in. This may sound like the advice of a killjoy, but in the end it will save you much suffering. Not only that, repeating the mantram at such times actually allows you to enjoy these moments in freedom, for when the mind is extremely excited, it is too busy swinging to and fro to be able to find joy.

When fortune smiles on you, when everyone agrees with you, when you get an unexpected opportunity to do something you like, these are all times you can repeat the mantram. When you hear good news, the mantram will consolidate your joy. When someone praises you, repeating the mantram will keep the praise from going to your head. Then, when someone criticizes you—as they must, sooner or later, because that is the nature of life—you will be able to consider the criticism objectively and not get depressed over it. If the praise is warranted, you can be appreciative; if the criticism is valid, you should act on it; but under no circumstances should you let praise or blame throw you into agitation. This is where the mantram comes to your rescue.

Looking forward too much to some kind of excitement in the future is another way of courting depression. Some of my friends tell me that as children they used to look forward so much to opening their presents on Christmas morning that they could hardly sleep the night before. Then, as soon as they opened the last package, depression began to set in. A few well-chosen presents for our children at Christmas are an appropriate way of showing love, especially if they are presents which we have made ourselves. But if we really love our children, we will do our very best not to let them get excited about the future and what it will bring them. Not only will this guard them against the depression that is sure to follow; it will help them develop a capacity for joy that is not subject to disappointment.

When we mortgage the present for the future, we are not only asking for depression in the future; we are also deadening ourselves to the present. Just see how many of us, if there is a big party to go to in the evening, go through our work that day with one eye on the clock, thinking, "Only six hours more; only five and a half hours more." We can wish away the whole week looking forward to a weekend of skiing; we can wish away the whole year looking forward to a vacation. And when we go on saying, "I can't wait to be twenty-one," or to get married, or to get promoted, or to retire, we can wish away an entire life.

With vacations, for example, we work for fifty weeks at our jobs looking forward to two exciting weeks in Acapulco or the Bahamas. All our expectation is on those two weeks, so our job seems like drudgery; our home life is humdrum. Expectation mounts as the vacation draws near: we plan, we pack, we talk. Then for two frantic weeks we are determined to have a good time, even if it kills us. When we get back, there should be an ambulance waiting to take us to the intensive care unit. All we have to show for this is a few slides, a bad sunburn, and a towel from the Hotel Ritz. We go back to our same old routine, which seems duller than ever, and soon we are looking forward to next year's vacation. I respond much more to Mahatma Gandhi's idea of a vacation. He was asked by a Western journalist, "Mr. Gandhi, you have been working fifteen hours a day, seven days a week, for fifty years. Why don't you take a vacation?" Gandhi's reply was, "I am always on vacation." We can make every day a vacation by getting away from preoccupation with ourselves and our own personal satisfactions. We learn to do this by thinking more of the needs of others and by repeating the mantram in order to keep our mind even, to shed our likes and dislikes, and to drop our problems at will. In doing this, we are banishing boredom and depression from our life completely.

Getting Out of a Depression

If you do not try these steps, or if you resort to them too late and find yourself in a depression, all is not lost; there are a number of things you can do to pull yourself out. Depression is simply dwelling on oneself—

one's problems, one's failures, one's inadequacies—and if you can distract the ego from this favorite pastime, you will find that you are no longer depressed.

One of the most important steps is not to spend any time trying to analyze your depression to see how it came about. This just feeds the depression, and even if you are able to pinpoint a cause, the depression will still be with you. In fact, the more you think about the causes, the more depressed you are likely to be. You can read any number of books on depression and the story will still be the same. But when you are in a depression, it doesn't really matter what the cause is, any more than it matters at the time what made your car go into a skid. The important thing is that the mind, like the car, is out of control, and that you need to act immediately in order to get control of it again. In other words, in both cases, the problem is mechanical.

Here, until you gain real mastery over your mind, the direct approach simply will not work. You cannot say, "I know I'm only depressed because I didn't get that raise, so I hereby shake this depression off"; the mind will only laugh at you. Instead, whenever you are tempted to think about how depressed you are and why, try repeating the mantram. When you can give your full attention to the mantram, there will be no attention left for your problems, which means that the depression has packed its bags and left town. At the beginning you will find this very difficult to do; the mind will slip away from the mantram again and again. But keep on trying; after a while the mantram will take hold, which means that the car of your mind is back on the road again and ready to come under control.

In fighting depression the mantram needs all the help it can get, and here the most effective support we can offer is to throw ourselves into work or activities that turn our attention outward and keep us from thinking about ourselves. The harder and more challenging the job is, the better, especially if it benefits those around you. Hard physical work is excellent, and it is particularly effective in the company of other people. As you cultivate the precious capacity to turn your attention outwards like this and to give your full attention to something that benefits others, depression will find you a less and less attractive host. Eventually it will give you up altogether and say, "Let me go find someone who is prepared to pay me the attention I am used to having."

Unfortunately, when people are depressed they usually do just the opposite of this. They hide themselves in their room, draw the curtains, and minimize the distractions so that they can dwell completely on themselves. Often they will say, "We don't want to inflict our depression on others." This may be a commendable motive for withdrawing, but it only makes the depression worse.

In India I once had a friend who used to withdraw this way when depression struck him. He was a very cultured, prosperous man and quite an entertaining person to be with, a good conversationalist and very hospitable—until he fell into a depression. For months he would go on being his usual entertaining self; then, abruptly, he would fall into a depression. He wouldn't talk to anyone in a civil manner; he wouldn't come out of his house; he wouldn't invite anyone in. This, too, used to go on for months. At last, when he was in the midst of one of these terrible depressions, I went to his house to see him. He had instructed his butler to tell callers that he was not at home, but I knew that he was; so before the butler could shut the door, I had slipped inside and started for my friend's room. I couldn't believe that it was the same man. His features were frozen in self-hatred, and he had nothing but hostility toward the whole world. He was furious when he saw me, and began using some strong language to drive me out. When he saw that words couldn't drive me out, he actually pushed me out the door. Now, I knew that this was not really my friend; it was just some virus that had taken control of him— and I knew how to deal with it, too. So I pushed my way back in, and I was able to stay and talk to him and finally help him. Afterwards he used to boast to people, "I even pushed him out of my house, but he cared so much for me that he came right back in."

Another bit of advice for coping with depression is simple but extremely powerful: always act as if you were not depressed. People in a depression walk slowly, with their heads down; they slump in their chairs with a preoccupied look in their eyes. They avoid being with people, and when they have to be with people they avoid talking to them or meeting their eyes. They may be so absorbed in themselves that they do not even see or hear what is going on around them. So when you are in a depression, make every effort to be with people and let them draw you out. Walk briskly with your head up; take an interest in what is going on around you, and smile at people and talk to them even if you don't feel like it. Before you know it, you will find that you are not pretending to be cheerful any longer; you really *are* cheerful, because you have forgotten yourself. Of course, it takes a certain amount of will to turn outward like this when everything inside you is crying to withdraw. But here again the mantram can come to your rescue; it will strengthen your will and enable you to remember that depression is just a habit which can be unlearned just as it was learned.

Spontaneity

Sometimes when I offer this advice people tell me, "That sounds artificial. Isn't it being dishonest to act differently from how you feel? I don't want to be artificial; I want to be natural and spontaneous. I don't want to be hypocritical; I want to be true to myself." We are not being hypocritical when we act cheerful; we are being hypocritical when we give in to depression or any other negative mental state. Depression is not our real condition; it is only a mask. Our real nature is abiding joy.

Everyone wants to be spontaneous these days, but very few seem to realize what spontaneity really is. Most of us act as if spontaneity means "doing your own thing": doing just what we like, when we like, and in the way we like. If the sky is blue and the sun is warm, we skip our classes or call our place of work to say that we won't be coming in. If we don't like a friend's new coat, we say so; after all, it's a free country, isn't it? We abandon ourselves to excitement on any pretext, and we fall into depression at the drop of a hat.

What we are pleased to call "spontaneity" here, if I may be blunt, is simply doing what we feel like doing and not doing what we don't feel like doing. When we live this way, we are really no more spontaneous than a rubber ball which bounces when we drop it on the sidewalk; we are simply reacting as we have been conditioned to react. Real spontaneity lies in being able to overcome years of wrong conditioning in order to express the abiding joy and infinite love which is our real nature. We are being truly spontaneous when we can change the habits of a lifetime overnight and not be oppressed by it. We are being truly spontaneous when we are able to drop our pet project and work for the welfare of those around us without a ripple of protest in the mind. We are being truly spontaneous when we can respond calmly, constructively, and compassionately to others when they are hostile to us.

It is not possible to attain spontaneity by doing only what we like, or postponing disagreeable jobs, or moving away from people who irritate us. When we do this, we are just drifting through life, following the course of least resistance. The Compassionate Buddha describes the spiritual life as "going against the current"—learning to go against all our wrong conditioning. By just drifting, we will never cross the sea of life to the far shore of abiding joy.

This "drifting" approach to spontaneous living reminds me of the little vegetable garden I planted when I first came to Berkeley. I didn't know anything about gardening, but one of my friends, a congenial Englishman, offered me advice and support. He was of the spontaneous school of gardening: the garden can take care of itself; you just put the seeds in the ground and come back in a few months to gather in the harvest. When I suggested that perhaps I should weed a little too, he used to tell me, "The weeds deserve their chance too, old boy." This was certainly an easy way to garden—effortless, in fact—but when autumn came, all that I harvested was one small ear of corn and a couple of shriveled tomatoes. This is exactly what happens with the garden of the mind. If we just let it grow any old way, we will get a bumper harvest of weeds, thistles, and brambles. But if we take care to cultivate wisely and weed out what is not so wise, our effort will produce a rich harvest in more abundant vitality, deeper personal relationships, and the resilience to face any challenge life may bring our way.

The secret of spontaneity is training; this is how we undo our conditioning. Look at the effortless grace with which a great artist or a great athlete performs. They make the most amazing feat look so simple that we think we all could do it, but we know that behind all their ease and grace are years of dedication, practice, and sustained effort. No one expects to be able to step onto the court at Wimbledon the first time she picks up a tennis racquet, or to play Beethoven's concerto in Carnegie Hall the first time he picks up a violin. It is just the same with the mind. We cannot just decide to be spontaneous; we cannot change our likes and dislikes or banish depression from our lives overnight; but we can all make these marvelous transformations in our consciousness if we are prepared to put in the sustained effort they require.

Any effort we make to keep the mind steady helps on all fronts. If we can drop our work at will, we will be much less liable to depression. If we can bear with those who irritate us, we will find it easier not to postpone necessary jobs. If we can juggle with our likes and dislikes, we can easily drop our work and even our problems at will. And whenever we repeat the mantram, we are helping to keep the mind calm and steady, which helps us to do everything in greater freedom. Even if we do nothing more than try to keep the mind steady during the ups and downs of the day, we are deepening our awareness of life far more than we know.

Harnessing Fear, Anger, and Greed ❧

When the Bible says, "As a man thinketh in his heart, so is he," it is telling us that the key to intentional living is in gaining mastery over the mind. The Compassionate Buddha puts the same message very precisely in the famous Twin Verses:

> All that we are is the result of what we have thought;
>> we are formed and molded by our thoughts.
> The man whose mind is shaped by selfish thoughts
>> causes misery whenever he speaks or acts.
> Sorrow follows him as the wheel follows
>> the foot of the bull that draws the cart.
>
> All that we are is the result of what we have thought;
>> we are formed and molded by our thoughts.
> The man whose mind is shaped by selfless thoughts
>> gives joy whenever he speaks or acts.
> Joy follows him like a shadow that never leaves him.

"Thought" here is not just the thoughts we think

with the conscious mind. It includes the workings of the unconscious as well, our fears and desires and worries and loves and aspirations. Most of the time, the vast majority of us live on the surface level of consciousness, not suspecting the storms that rage in our unconscious. We get some hint of the tremendous power of these storms when they break through to the surface in the form of fear, anger, and greed. When these get out of control, they can pick us up and hurl us about as they like, exactly as if some force takes us over and makes us do things, say things, that we would not ordinarily do.

Take fear, for example. Fear of snakes is part of our consciousness in rural India; when a villager is walking home in the twilight and sees a snake on the path ahead of him—it may not even be a real snake, just a bit of coiled-up rope—he gives a jump that would make any Olympic athlete envious. If he had stood calmly and said, "Let me see how far I can jump," he would not have been able to cover even half that distance. Fear gives him access to a deeper level of consciousness, where he finds the power to jump.

Fear plays a valuable role here if it enables the villager to avoid being bitten by the snake, but most of the time fear, anger, and greed serve no useful purpose. They are simply power going to waste—or worse, power being used destructively. If we take an honest look at our behavior under the influence of fear or anger or the compulsion of greed, we have to admit that it is not very pretty; it is not something we are very proud of. Here is where the mantram is an invaluable ally. It can harness all this destructive power that is going to waste and transform it: fear into fearlessness, anger into compassion, and greed into the desire to be of service to those around us. It is very much like harnessing a river. Where formerly floods used to ruin crops and destroy whole villages, the same river once harnessed now makes the crops flourish and generates power to light people's homes.

The simplest thing to do when you are caught by fear, anger, or greed is to go for a long, fast walk repeating the mantram. This may sound simplistic, but try it. Go for a fast walk repeating *Rama, Rama, Rama* or *Jesus, Jesus, Jesus* in your mind, and you will find that the relationship between the rhythm of your breathing, the rhythm of your footsteps, and the rhythm of the mantram has a deep influence on your consciousness. Recently a friend of mine told me she had discovered that when she was upset, if she could hold on to the mantram for twenty minutes while she walked, it could transform any negative emotion. "When I realized that," she said, "I realized that any transformation is possible." You may not always be able to afford the luxury of going for a fast walk, but you can repeat the mantram any time. With practice you will find that when some negative emotion rises like a tidal wave in your mind, you don't have to be flung up onto the beach or pounded down against the bottom of the sea as in the old days; you can ride the wave on the mantram board with your arms spread wide. Once you have learned this skill, there is a tremendous sense of mastery.

Fear and anger and greed agitate the mind; they churn the mind up like a stormy sea. When your mind is heaving up and down, it may be difficult to hold on to the mantram if your mantram is long. For emergencies like this, I would recommend using a shortened form of the mantram, the kernel of the mantram: *Rama* if your mantram is *Hare Rama Hare Rama, Om* if it is *Om mani padme hum, Jesus* if you use some form of the Jesus Prayer such as *Lord Jesus Christ* or *Lord Jesus Christ, have mercy on me*. This kernel of the mantram is the most potent word in the Holy Name; it is short and simple. No matter how agitated your mind is, you can hang on to it while it does its work of harnessing and transforming the power that was rampaging in you.

Fear

When you are afraid, repeat the mantram; it has the power to change fear into fearlessness. For people who claim that fear is not a problem for them, I simply ask if they have any worries. The usual answer is, "More than I can count." Worries are simply little fears; put a hundred worries together and you have one big fear. When your vitality leaks out through a hundred little worries, it is no wonder that you feel inadequate to the challenges of the day. So repeat the mantram when you are worried, and it will change worry into confidence. The same goes for the rest of fear's poor relations: the mantram protects you not only against worry, but also against anxiety, nervousness, and apprehension.

When I was at the University of Minnesota many years ago, where I spent the winter and lived to tell the tale, I had a young friend from my old state of Kerala whose finals were beginning. One subject was particularly difficult for him, and his scholarship depended on getting straight *A*'s. He was a good student, but as happens on the eve of finals, he became very anxious and his memory began to play tricks on him. He knocked on my door and asked if I had some immediate help for somebody who was facing a final exam. I have no objection to being made a last resort, and I didn't ask him about his spiritual beliefs or his philosophical background. I knew the tradition from which his family comes, so I gave him the mantram used in that tradition and took him for a walk from Minne-

153

apolis to Saint Paul and back again, along the banks of the Mississippi River, six miles to and six miles fro. Every time he would say, "I'm tired; can't we stop?" I would tell him, "Just keep repeating your mantram." When we got back to the dormitory, he was so completely relaxed that I just opened the door and pushed him in; he went straight in and fell into his bed and slept soundly. As I said, he had been a good student, so he went to his finals the next morning rested and with a quiet assurance and did very well.

Many different things can make us anxious, and this anxiety expresses itself in so many ways. When you have to speak on the platform, if you are not used to it, you see what interesting things can happen. Suddenly you will find your hands swelling. You try to put them in your pockets; they won't go in. Something happens to your larynx, you have strange flutterings in your stomach, a little mouse seems to be running up and down your spinal column, and your legs turn to rubber. These are all experiences which many aspiring speakers have undergone, and one of the easiest remedies is to repeat the mantram. When you go for a job interview and you get the butterfly effect, instead of indulging in that little last-minute fussing ritual with your tie, try the mantram. When you go to the dentist, or to the doctor, or to a hospital, these are all occasions to repeat the mantram. Use the mantram when you are in pain; it will take your mind off the pain, whereas fear only makes pain worse. When you are fearful and keep dwelling on yourself, that naturally impedes the healing process, but when you switch your mind over to the mantram, your body is able to go about its work of healing unimpeded.

When you are faced with a really big fear, it can unify your consciousness, and at a time like this, the mantram can go in very deep. A friend of mine works as a nurse in the intensive care unit of a local hospital, and she had as a patient an elderly woman who was seriously ill, so ill that she wasn't even able to breathe except with the aid of one of those breathing machines, a resuscitator. The patient was a Catholic, so my friend suggested that she repeat *Hail Mary*. She began doing it and her condition improved greatly. In this case, the mantram helped more than anything else that had been tried; even the doctor expressed his appreciation.

Unfortunately, there are people who remember the mantram when they are afraid but stop using it when the danger is past. We have a story in India about how a person crossing a shaky bridge says *Rama, Rama, Rama* for all he is worth, but as soon as he is back on terra firma again it is *kama, kama, kama—kama* stands for selfish desires. Many people are like this. It would be better to have been using the mantram all along;

then, in the face of great fear, the mantram will be right there at your side, reminding you that the Lord is your protector.

Anger

Whenever I talk about using the mantram to transform fear and anger, people nod approvingly as long as I am talking about fear. After all, no one wants to be fearful; no one wants to worry. But the nods of approval often stop when I ask people to repeat the mantram in moments of anger. "You're not asking us to repress anger?" they ask. "Isn't it better to express anger than to repress it?" This is a legitimate question, but it is based on the assumption that we have only two choices where anger is concerned: expression or repression. Either way, anger eventually works against us, undermining our relationships, our security, and even our health. But there is a third alternative: we can transform anger, through the repetition of the mantram. Anger is power, and the mantram can transform this negative power into its positive counterpart, which is compassion. Not only that, the very power that is behind anger serves to drive the mantram even deeper into our consciousness.

Anger is so endemic today that our century could be called the age of anger. There is even a cult surrounding anger, which conditions us to regard the angry person as powerful and dynamic and free. This is how anger is shown in books, in movies, on television, everywhere, and we have come to believe it. There are workshops now where people are taught to express their anger more freely, where they are taught that when someone gets angry with them, the way to gain control of the situation is to get angry in return. In fact, in our day, anger is considered to be part of expressing oneself, a vital means of communication.

But if you have the detachment, take a good look at what anger actually does. When someone gets angry with you and you get angry in return, is this really expressing yourself, or are you just dancing to the tune they are calling? And the angry words that you hurl at your partner, or your parents, or your children—even if you think they clear the air, they will only rankle for a long time in the other person's consciousness, which scarcely contributes to better personal relations.

All too often it is with those we are emotionally entangled with that we get angry: they are nearby, so we lash out. If getting angry actually cemented personal relations, I would be all for it. But this anger only drives a wedge into the relationship, and each time we get angry we are making the split deeper and deeper. The words we say in anger, the decisions we make in anger, the things we do in anger—none of these are likely to be wise. There is a chilling statistic that over seventy percent of murder victims are friends or relatives of the murderer, slain in anger often over what started out as trifling quarrels—and often, ironically, with firearms that were in the house to protect the occupants from intruders from outside.

Finally, see what damage the angry person is doing to himself. My Grandmother used to say that getting angry was like swallowing a lighted firecracker. The angry person may hurl barbed words and even throw things, but it is he who really gets hurt—by developing serious physical problems like asthma, ulcers, high blood pressure, heart disease, and even cancer. When you keep letting yourself get angry, you wear an anger rut in your consciousness; the anger response becomes habitual. You have become anger-prone, and anger-prone people, wherever they go in life, will always find some obliging person to step on their corns or contradict their pet opinion. For such people, steadfast relationships and emotional security become impossible.

There is a tremendous statement in the Hindu scriptures: "That which makes you sick, if harnessed, can be that which makes you well." When I say that anger makes us sick, it is not an exaggeration, and I am pleased to see that the medical profession is slowly coming around to this view of anger. In a medical journal not long ago I read an excellent article by an American doctor titled "The Therapeutic Value of

Charity"—charity in the New Testament sense of love, forbearance, forgiveness. This doctor cites a number of case histories of men and women who developed some very serious physical problems after prolonged bouts of anger and resentment, including strokes and heart attacks precipitated by violent outbursts of temper. This is anger making us sick. But when we can harness the power in anger, the same power that was making us ill can give us the capacity to work tirelessly to relieve the distress of those around us. Health and security come our way on both the physical and the emotional level when we forget ourselves in working for some selfless goal.

Gandhi provides a perfect example of how anger harnessed can give us access to the resources locked deep within us. In 1893, Mohandas Karamchand Gandhi was a young, inexperienced Indian lawyer in South Africa. His employer, a well-to-do businessman, had bought him a first-class ticket on the train to Pretoria on business. Gandhi had not been settled in his seat for too long when another passenger, a European, entered. He took one look at Gandhi's brown skin and left immediately, only to return with the conductor, who demanded that Gandhi move to a third-class car. Gandhi refused, and was roughly thrown from the train onto the railway platform at a place called Maritzburg, high in the mountains, where he spent the night on the cold railway platform deep in thought. It was, he said later, the turning point in his career. He was full of anger, partly because of this personal injustice but more because it was just one of countless such injustices suffered every day by black Africans and Indians in South Africa. After a long inner struggle, Gandhi resolved not to rest until he had set these injustices right, not by violence or retaliation but through the loving power of nonviolent resistance, which elevates the consciousness of both oppressed and oppressor.

An angry man is allowing power to rise against him and enslave him, but when he learns to control this tremendous source of power, he can use it to meet any challenge and to make his greatest contribution to those around him. Here it is that I value Gandhi's example very much, because it shows that we all have the choice to undertake this transformation ourselves. This was pointed out with keen insight by the Compassionate Buddha. When people used to go to him complaining that they were upset, telling him, "Our children upset us; our partner agitates us," his simple reply would be, "You are not upset because of your children or your partner; you are upset because you are upsettable." The choice is ours to make ourselves unsettable.

The simple solution I would suggest to the problem of anger is repetition of the mantram. This is how we can become slow to anger and quick to forgive. Do not wait until you have developed a full-blown rage, when judgment is clouded and the mind is heaving up and down; it will be very difficult to hang on to the mantram then, or even to remember it. Try to remember the mantram as soon as you feel anger beginning to rise, when the first storm warnings are out. If possible, go out for a fast walk repeating the mantram. I need hardly add here that you are much more likely to remember the mantram at times like this if you have been using it regularly throughout your day.

Anger doesn't always appear on the stage of our consciousness with a red face and flaring nostrils; it also takes the form of resentment. Slow, burning resentments consume as much of our vital capital as outbursts of anger do, and they can just as surely poison a relationship, too. When we nurse them and dwell on them, resentments can wear a groove in our consciousness just like a broken record. When we resent a person, for whatever reason, we find more and more things to be resentful about, and when we go on like this, this broken record of resentments can be set off just by the sound of that person's voice, or even by a car the same color as theirs. Even if you can't remember the mantram when you are angry, you can always use it when you are resentful. Instead of repeating the same old resentment over and over, substitute the Holy Name. I believe that it was Thomas Jefferson who said, "When you are angry, count to ten before you speak." I would say, when you are angry, repeat the mantram ten times before you speak; when you are very angry, repeat it a hundred times, and when you are resentful, just keep on repeating it as long as you can.

Impatience is another of anger's poor relations. We can hardly wait for the other person to get out of our way so we can do what we want; we can hardly wait for him to finish his sentence so that we can speak. I still get taken aback to hear drivers honking their horns when the car ahead of them doesn't move the instant the traffic light turns green. Patience, on the other hand, is one of the most marvelous qualities in life. With patience we can bear with others despite their drawbacks; we can support them even when they make mistakes and still point out these mistakes lovingly and constructively. When we practice patience, we are responding to the real person, not to the mask of greed or anger that he or she is wearing. Patience is an unfailing remedy for friction in personal relations, and one given us long ago in the beautiful line from Proverbs, "A soft answer turneth away wrath." Even if a person has never won a beauty contest, has no money in the bank, can't even change a flat tire, if he or she has inexhaustible patience, then we will find that life with such a person will never grow stale.

It is in personal relations that we have the greatest opportunity to reduce our self-will and grow to our full stature. Here the cultivation of patience is one of the most effective ways to improve relations with our family and friends and everyone else with whom we come in contact. When disciples used to ask the Buddha, "How do we become more patient?" he would reply, "By trying to become more patient." We don't develop patience by wishing that we were more patient, or by wearing a button which says, *I Am Patient*; we learn patience by trying. I once asked my Grandmother why there should be people to criticize me and attack me, and she replied, "How else can you learn patience?"

There is a proverb in my mother tongue: "It takes two to get married and two to quarrel." When someone criticizes you or contradicts you or speaks to you in an unpleasant tone of voice, there is no quarrel as long as you remember that you have the choice not to reply in the same manner. There is trouble only when we react on the stimulus and response level of tit for tat, which may be all right for two-year-olds but not for mature men and women. It takes two to quarrel: the other person can throw down the gauntlet, but we don't have to pick it up. If we can remember the mantram at such times, it will help us to be more patient, and our example will help the other person to be more patient too.

To do this, it helps immensely to slow down. It is difficult to be patient with others when you're in a tearing hurry yourself. Also, of course, it helps to remember that everyone has a point of view. But most important of all, repeat the mantram. When a flood of impatient words is rising, shut your mouth and keep saying the mantram; let the harsh words dash themselves against the back of your teeth if they have to, but don't let them out. Even if you think that you'll jump out of your skin if that car ahead doesn't leap into motion a split second after the light turns green, keep repeating the mantram. It will keep your hand off the horn and your blood pressure down, and best of all, it will transform the rising power of impatience into that most precious of qualities, patience.

Greed

Greed is another of the undesirable weeds which we can root out of our consciousness through the use of the mantram. I use "greed" here to stand for selfish desire in all its varied forms: the greed for personal power, for prestige, for profit, for pleasure; the belief that we can find abiding happiness in pursuing our own selfish satisfactions regardless of the cost to those around us.

Let me stress that what I am deprecating here is not desire, but *selfish* desire. An unselfish desire to alleviate the suffering of those around us, or to contribute to the welfare of those around us, is the highest of human motivations. Mahatma Gandhi, who worked with no thought of personal power or prestige or profit, was once asked by a European reporter, "Don't you have any ambition?" He replied, "On the contrary, I am the most ambitious of men: I want to reduce myself to zero." In other words, he wanted to eliminate all selfish desires completely. A selfish desire for my own personal profit, for example, can be transformed into a selfless desire to see that everyone has shelter, clothing, and enough to eat; it is just a matter of spiritual engineering. So when I use the word *greed,* I am referring to selfish desire.

Action motivated by greed is not likely to be in our own best interests, or in the best interests of others, and in the end it will leave us unsatisfied and alienated. When we are driven by greed, it is as if we go through life wearing blinders which enable us to see only through a little slit. The man who is driven by greed for money, for example, looks at the world through a slit shaped like a dollar sign; when he looks at a sunny meadow all he is thinking is, "I could make a mint building a subdivision here."

We have all been conditioned to believe that by

fulfilling our desires we will find lasting satisfaction. Suppose the desire for a burgundy cherry ice cream cone arises in your mind, and you go buy one and eat it. If I ask you just then, "Are you satisfied?" you will assure me that you are. But if I ask an hour later, "Does that burgundy cherry cone still bring you some satisfaction?" you will say, "That was an hour ago." With penetrating insight, the mystics will tell us that when we have a desire for a certain thing, a certain experience, and we fulfill that desire, the happiness we feel is not something given by that thing or that experience; it is due to having no craving for a little while. It is not because this craving has been satisfied, but because for just a little while there is a state of no craving.

But the mind does not rest long in this state of no desire. The mind is a factory manufacturing desires in all makes and models and colors, working overtime seven days a week. With that first bite of burgundy cherry ice cream, you shut your eyes and let your taste buds rejoice, but by the time you are halfway through the cone, you are already thinking about a cup of coffee or the shoe sale next door.

It is the nature of a desire to exhaust itself, the mystics say. Even if eating that burgundy cherry cone gives you satisfaction—and no one is denying that—how long does this satisfaction last? More than that, if you keep on eating ice cream, cone after cone, satisfaction soon turns to satiation, and then eventually to revulsion. But this hasn't helped to get rid of the desire: when you are hungry again, the desire will be back, and no amount of indulgence on the physical level can root it out, because desire is in the mind.

There is much more satisfaction in resisting a wrong desire than in yielding to it. I once enabled a woman to give up smoking just by telling her this; she was responsive to my concern and she had the capacity to accept the challenge my words implied. A great many people would gladly quit smoking, a habit which mounting evidence on all sides shows to be extremely harmful, if they only had the will. Perhaps you have tried to give up smoking: suddenly something will remind you of tobacco and the desire for a cigarette rises in your mind. If you give in to this desire, you are not likely to succeed in giving up smoking, and when the cigarette is gone, you will be left with that shabby feeling that all your good resolves have come to naught. At times like these, use the mantram to strengthen your will. Desires are short-lived; at first the desire will loom over you like a tiger, but if you can hold out for just a little while by repeating the mantram, you will see the desire shrink to the size of a mouse and scurry out under the door. You may not have seen the last of the tiger, but after a few experiences like this, you gain confidence that the mantram *will* reduce that tiger to a mouse, and finally seal up the mousehole in the bargain.

The Chandogya Upanishad gives us a penetrating insight into the nature of desire when it says, "There is no joy in the finite; there is joy only in the infinite." What we are all looking for is unending joy, a delight that never pales or cloys. But if we try to find this unending joy on the physical level, where it is the very nature of things to change, then we have lost it. I have known some very wealthy people, some famous people, some people who have indulged in all of the pleasures that life has to offer. When I have asked them very candidly whether they have found what they are looking for, they confide, if they are honest and sensitive: "What we were looking for seems to have slipped through our fingers."

In the wise words of Jesus, lay up your treasure in heaven, where thieves cannot steal it and rust cannot corrupt it. In my understanding, this means becoming aware of the indivisible unity of life. The joy of knowing that all life is one and that every day you have worked to enrich the lives of those around you is a joy that never ends. This is our real inheritance, but we cannot claim it as long as we spend our time looking for a few cents of prestige or profit or a few dollars of pleasure.

I have observed that young people today are remarkably free from greed for power and profit, but they make up for this in the great faith they put in pleasure. The pursuit of pleasure has become a cult today, and not only with the young. This is partly our deep belief that in gratifying our senses we can become beautiful and fulfilled, and partly our wrong conditioning by the mass media, which is now in the very air we breathe. And nowhere has the pursuit of pleasure caused more unhappiness and more broken relationships than in the matter of sex.

The sex drive is a tremendously powerful force. On the physical level it brings two people together; on the spiritual level, when harnessed, this same power can bring us together into union with all life. In other words, sex is sacred. It has a beautiful place in a loyal and loving relationship between man and woman, where it can bring them even closer together. But sex without loyalty eventually disrupts a relationship, and on no account will it help us physically, psychologically, or spiritually to indulge this impulse indiscriminately as the mass media are urging us to do.

This is not moralizing, but simply pointing out that when a relationship is based entirely on the physical level, on physical appeal, that appeal will eventually exhaust itself. It is a law just like Newton's law of gravity. If a relationship is not founded on mutual love and respect—and let me point out that we have to work at this day by day by putting the needs of the other person before our own—then when the physical appeal goes, the relationship *has* to fall apart. Now Juliet thrills even to hold Romeo's hand, but in a few months that same hand will feel clammy. Romeo is charmed by the way Juliet tosses her head, but all too soon the very same gesture will only irritate him. The tendency here is to blame the other person, or to say, "Oh, well, I guess it just didn't work out." When we do this, we go through life never suspecting that we cannot build a lasting relationship on the physical level, and we find ourselves enacting the same drama over and over. Romeo has just broken up with Juliet; he looks at Ophelia and is captivated by the way *she* tosses her head, and off he goes again.

Desire is in the mind. Indulging a desire gives some temporary satisfaction, but as we find out to our cost, that very same desire will soon be back in a stronger form. Sometimes friends confide in me that after years of dwelling on sex, they think of it almost constantly. When the desire for sensory satisfaction becomes this powerful, it seems a little oppressive. Very few people realize what mastery there is in being able to let a desire arise at the proper time and to keep it still at other times. We lose nothing in this. It is the person who constantly dwells on sense pleasures and indulges in them indiscriminately whose senses become tired and jaded; the man or woman who gains some mastery over the thinking process finds that the senses have become faithful servants. This is not bleaching the color out of life; it is gaining mastery over life.

A tremendous amount of vital energy is consumed in thinking about sense pleasures—fantasizing about them, talking about them, remembering old scenes and old faces. Think how high your electric bill would be at the end of the month if you left your lights on all the time. That is why we have switches, to turn off the lights when we don't need them on. It is very much the same with sexual desire. The mantram helps us to get at the switch in our mind, so that we can conserve all this energy and put it to use wisely and selflessly. One young friend told me that the reason he played tennis was that a good, concentrated game of tennis was the only thing which would take his mind off sex. This is one way to keep from dwelling on sex, but it is not without its practical problems. Try the mantram instead; you won't need a racquet, you won't need a special costume, and you will have something to fall back on even if it's raining or the tennis court is under ten inches of snow. You can use the mantram any time, under any circumstances.

There is another very practical reason for using

the mantram to conserve and transform greed: it can save us a great deal of suffering later on. In the second chapter of the Bhagavad Gita, one of the best loved and most practical of the scriptures in the rich spiritual heritage of Hinduism, we are told:

"When you keep thinking about sense objects, attachment comes. Attachment breeds desire, the lust of possession which, when thwarted, burns to anger. Anger clouds the judgment and robs you of the power to learn from past mistakes. Lost is the discriminative faculty, and your life is utter waste."

It makes much more sense to deal with this problem at the beginning of this chain of events instead of waiting until things have reached unmanageable proportions. The old proverb "A stitch in time saves nine" embodies a good deal of native wisdom. The stitch which will save nine is not to keep thinking about sense objects in the first place, and here the mantram is invaluable.

From my university teaching days, I recall an incident which illustrates how desire can drive us to action. I had a colleague in the physics department who was completely devoted to research work. He was never without his coffee, from which I gathered that coffee and research work go together. In fact, he was always in his chair with his journals and his slide rule;

he never used to go for walks, and I had seldom seen him very active. One day, when I was coming back after a late show a mile from the campus, I saw him walking by the movie theater. I was astonished; I thought he had forgotten how to walk. "What made you throw yourself out of your chair like this and walk all this way?" I asked him. "You're breaking the habits of a lifetime." "Coffee," he muttered. "I ran out of coffee. I knew I could get some near here even at this hour." So I asked, "Why didn't you just stay at your desk and keep working?" "I couldn't concentrate," he said. "No matter what I read, all I could think about was coffee. Thermodynamics turned into coffee; Planck's constant turned into coffee; everything turned into coffee. I just had to get some." This is the power that is locked up in our desires. If just this little desire for a cup of coffee—not exactly the strongest of our addictions—can have so much power, how much more power must there be in a really strong desire, such as sex? Of course, I took advantage of the occasion to tell my friend that that is the time to repeat the mantram, because when you have a powerful urge, it acts like a hammer: *coffee, coffee, coffee.* If you can change *coffee, coffee, coffee* to *Rama, Rama, Rama* or *Jesus, Jesus, Jesus,* that same power will be used to drive the Holy Name into your consciousness. This is true for all negative emotions. Fear is a hammer,

173

anger a sledge hammer, and any self-centered desire a real pile driver.

Desire is power which we can harness or let go to waste. We have all been given this power for one purpose: to realize the indivisible unity of life; as the Buddha would put it, to cross from this shore of separateness to the far shore of unity. It is a little like crossing from Berkeley to San Francisco. Some people drive straight to the freeway and over the bridge to the other shore. Other people are like those trucks you see with the words *Frequent Stops* on the back: they stop for a pizza, they stop to see what is on sale at the Coop, they stop to see what an old friend is up to. Such people will never make it to the freeway; they won't reach the other shore before night comes. Now, we all have a certain margin of error for making a few stops. Experimenting with the toys of life and finding that they don't fully satisfy us is part of growing up. But when we keep on making stops all our life, it is tragic. Then, even if after many years we get a glimpse of the purpose of life, we may not have the fuel left to make the journey.

A tremendous amount of power can be locked up in our desires, particularly when they have become compulsive. This is like driving with the emergency brake on: it diminishes our vital energy, our ability to respond to others and to be sensitive to their needs.

If we could release this power, it could be harnessed for the benefit of all. There is no need to despair if you have come to let your life be ruled by compulsive desires, by compulsive patterns of talking, acting, thinking, or relating to people. You can use the mantram to release all this trapped power. Each time the thought of the compulsion comes up, repeat the mantram—and of course, don't act on the compulsion, either; the mantram will help in this too. Eventually the very thought of the compulsion will remind you of the mantram, and then you see the light at the end of the tunnel. People sometimes ask how it is that afterwards the mantram doesn't bring up the thought of the compulsion. The mantram is so much greater than the compulsion that it swallows up the compulsion without a trace. After some experience, your associations with the mantram will not be of all the troubles it has saved you from, but rather of deeper devotion and faith in its power.

The Compassionate Buddha points out with penetrating insight that we are not punished for our sins; we are punished by our sins. Many people these days are allergic to the notion of sin and punishment. They rebel against the idea of some external tribunal meting out punishment for infractions of a law to which they may not even subscribe. So instead, I like to talk about mistakes and consequences—it is the same. We are all prepared to admit that if we make a mistake, we have to accept the consequences. If I use a knife carelessly, I cut myself; there is nothing unjust about this, nothing which violates human dignity. Similarly, being subject to fear, or anger, or greed is its own punishment. When you keep getting angry, the punishment is nothing imposed from outside: anger is its own punishment in the damage it does to our health, our emotional security, and our relationships with others. Whenever one of these negative emotions rises, if you can remember the mantram, you are reminding yourself of the unity of life. The Lord is standing at your side, and then what is there to fear, who is there to be angry against, who is there to possess or manipulate?

The Mantram at the
Time of Death ✿

Throughout our village my Grandmother was looked
up to as a source of great strength; so when death was
approaching, people used to send for her to sit beside
them and comfort them in their last hours. Sometimes
she would insist that I accompany her, even when I
was still a child. As I sat by the side of the dying while
my Grandmother held their hand, the sorrow and the
agony I witnessed used to torture me. In those days,
I didn't understand why she took me to these terrible
scenes, but their impact on my consciousness was profound. The question began to haunt me, "Is this going
to happen to me, too? Is there no way I can go beyond
death?"

Every morning my Grandmother used to go to
our ancestral temple for worship. On her return, she
would stick behind my ear a flower offered to the Lord
in worship and bless me with these simple words:
"May you be like Markandeya!" Markandeya was
a boy in the Hindu scriptures whose heart was filled

even from childhood with love for God. When death came to claim him in his sixteenth year, he sat down in deep meditation on the Lord, one of whose names in Sanskrit is Mrityunjaya, the Conqueror of Death. Realizing in the depths of his consciousness his unity with the Lord, Markandeya passed beyond the sway of death. This is a story familiar to every Hindu boy, so when I heard my Grandmother tell me every morning *May you be like Markandeya,* it sank very deep into me. By this constant reminder and by taking me to all those scenes of grief beside the dying, she made me aware of death and gave me the intense desire to go beyond it. More than that, she showed me that death could be transcended in this very life.

Everyone will agree that some day the body must grow old, decay, and drop away, but not many will face the fact that it will happen to them. The proof is that if a person really believes he will die, he will do something about it. If I may say so, very few understand the real significance of death. The purpose of death is to go beyond death, and we can use death itself to do this. When we realize fully that we are not this changing body but the changeless Self who dwells in the body, we conquer death here and now.

We hear a great deal about death these days; everywhere we look there are books and seminars on dying. This is a change for the better, because until recently death has been a forbidden topic in our society. When we draw a curtain around death, hiding it away out of sight in hospitals and rest homes, our lives can become shallow. But talking about death is only a first step. These books and seminars are intended to help us to accept death, but they do not show us how to go beyond it. Talking about death can be a real service if it enables people to shed the body more peacefully or more courageously, but the mantram can do this for us far more effectively than any book or seminar.

In India, it is the custom to sing the mantram beside a dying person. This helps to console those around, and it helps very much to steady the mind of the person who is about to die. We find similar practices in other traditions too. But it is even more effective for the person who is dying to repeat the mantram silently, in the mind. I have been by the side of dying people many times, and I can testify that this is of immense help. It banishes fear and confusion and can be a source of continuous consolation and support.

All the mystics tell us to live each moment as if it were our last, and the man or woman who repeats the mantram regularly and with real devotion is actually preparing for this. The person who has become established in the mantram, who has made the mantram an integral part of his or her consciousness, is prepared for death at all times. Mahatma Gandhi, explaining this state, said once that it would be easier for his life to stop than for his mantram *Rama* to cease reverberating in his consciousness. And this is indeed how it came to pass: when his body was pierced by the assassin's bullets, Gandhi blessed his attacker with folded hands and fell with *Rama* on his lips and in his heart.

If we are able to repeat the mantram at the moment of death, the great mystics tell us, we merge into the Lord just as a bursting bubble becomes one with the sea. This is not just a Hindu idea; we find it in all the other great religions too. I remember a friend once confiding in me how comforting he found it as a child when one of his teachers, a very loving nun, told him that he would go straight to heaven if he were saying the Hail Mary at the moment he died. We tend to forget as adults that children can often be deeply troubled by such questions, and this boy found himself more responsive than ever to the beautiful Hail Mary because it eased his fears and gave him some sense of control over his destiny.

The power of the mantram to unite us with the Lord at the moment of death is dramatized in India in a story of a rich and selfish merchant who thought of nothing but his own profit and pleasure. This man had only one child—a son, born to him late in life, of whom he was dotingly fond. As is frequently done, he had taken his son's name from the scriptures; the boy was called Narayana, "the perfect human being," a beautiful name for the Lord which reminds us that we become divine when all separateness is eradicated from our hearts.

As the years went by, this merchant became more and more alienated from those around him, and his attachment to his only son grew stronger. Finally he found himself on his deathbed, and through his mind went the thought of all the things that death was snatching from him: his business, his money, his house, his servants, his treasured possessions . . . . The King of Death appeared and approached his side, coming to take him. Then he realized that he would have to part even with his son Narayana, the only other human being in the world whom he loved. The agony of this was unbearable, and as the King of Death reached out for him, he cried out from the very bottom of his heart, "Narayana!"

At this moment the Lord appeared. "Take your hands off him," he told the King of Death; "he called on me with his dying breath." "I beg your pardon," the King of Death said, "but he didn't mean you; he meant that son of his that he can't bear to leave behind." "I know," the Lord replied, "but nonetheless he called my name, and anyone who calls on me in the very depths of his consciousness will surely be united with me, just as this man has become."

This idea that the mantram can be our salvation at the moment of death is not as simplistic as it may seem at first. It's not as if we can lead as selfish and sensate a life as we please until the very last second and then say the Holy Name and attain salvation. It is not possible to say the mantram with all our heart at the moment of death unless we have been repeating it for a long time before too. An English disciple once asked his spiritual teacher, Sri Ramana Maharshi, why he couldn't just throw himself under a train repeating the mantram and attain salvation without all those years of discipline. Sri Ramana Maharshi's penetrating answer was that his last thought would not be the mantram; it would be the "I" thought.

The process of death as described by the great mystics may throw some light on why this is so. Dying, they tell us, is a more complicated process than we ordinarily think. It is not sudden; it is a gradual withdrawal of consciousness from the body into the self. First, consciousness is withdrawn from the senses to the mind. The senses shut down, and outer awareness of the body and of our surroundings is gone. We still have ears, but we hear nothing because consciousness has been withdrawn; we still have eyes, but there is nothing outside that we see. Yet even though we can no longer see or hear, there is still consciousness in the mind, with all its desires and regrets, all its conflicts and hopes and fears. As long as we have these selfish desires, conflicts, and reservations, consciousness will remain in the mind at a deep level, where all desires and conflicts merge in the "I" thought at the time of death.

This process is strikingly parallel to what happens in deep meditation. When we are concentrating deeply, we will not hear the planes in the sky or the cars on the road, because we have withdrawn consciousness from the senses. The crucial difference is that in meditation this is a voluntary withdrawal, whereas in death it is involuntary; often it is even a tearing away. In meditation, however, we go even further: we deliberately seek to withdraw consciousness not only from the senses, but from the mind as well. This is what stilling the mind means.

To withdraw consciousness from the senses into the mind is not too hard, but it is very difficult to withdraw consciousness at will from the mind into the Self, into the core of purity and perfection which is at the very center of our being. Yet as long as the mind has not been stilled through the practice of meditation and the repetition of the mantram, consciousness will remain in the mind at the moment of death. We will still be identified with the ego, and our last thought will be *I, I, I.* To repeat the mantram at this stage is impossible if we have only been saying it on the surface level of consciousness, for there is no surface level any longer. To be able to repeat the mantram at the actual moment of death, the mantram must have sunk very, very deep into the mind—so deep that instead of our last thought being *I, I, I,* the last thought will be of the Lord, whose symbol is the mantram.

This has tremendous practical significance. If we have been living for ourselves, our last thought will be of ourselves, and there will be no way to avoid the suffering of ego-identification when the body is wrenched away. Abruptly, everything that we hold dear will be snatched away from us: our possessions, our cherished plans for the future, our loved ones, and even our body and the miscellaneous collection of likes and dislikes, habits and opinions that we are pleased to call our personality. Unless we have worked long and hard to cultivate detachment from all this— in other words, unless we have been trying to lead the spiritual life—the pain of this separation will be terrible. But if we have been repeating the mantram with sincerity and enthusiasm until it has become an integral part of our consciousness, even in life we can always be completely mindful of the deathless, change- less Reality we call God. Then, when the body is shed, our individual consciousness will merge in the Lord, who is our real and deepest Self.

In other words, even in life, the person who has

realized the indivisible unity of life has already died to all that was separate in him, all that was selfish in her, to come to life in the Lord. This is why Saint Francis says, "It is in dying that we are born to eternal life." This death of the ego is the purpose of all the disciplines of the spiritual life. Even in little things, whenever we are very patient or cheerfully do something we dislike, a little of our selfishness and self-will has died. Little by little we surrender everything—not under duress, but entirely by free choice, until we no longer need to hang on to anything outside us for support. Then, once we are established in this state of unity, we are established in it forever. This is what Jesus means when he offers us life everlasting: our constant awareness of the unity of life, our constant awareness of the Lord, is not interrupted even when the physical body dies.

My Grandmother, who was not intellectually oriented, had a rather different but very vivid way of getting this point across. I remember once asking her why death should involve so much suffering. She didn't answer directly; she just told me to go sit in a big wooden chair there in our ancestral home. "You hold on to this chair as hard as you can," she said. "I'm going to try to pull you out." I held on to the chair with all my might, and she began to pull. She was a strong woman, and when she started to pull I thought my arms were going to come off, but I held on for all I was worth. Finally, despite all my resistance, she wrenched me out of the chair. "That hurt, Granny," I said. "Let's try it again," she replied, "but this time don't hold on." I didn't, and there was no struggle, no pain; she raised me effortlessly and gracefully into her arms.

It was a very eloquent answer. Death is going to take our body anyway, no matter what we do, and the more we try to hang on to the body with all its desires and fears, the more we are going to suffer when death wrenches these things away. On the other hand, when we overcome identification with the body and ego through meditation and the repetition of the mantram, we know from direct spiritual experience that the body is not us, but only a jacket which we have been wearing all these years. Then, when the jacket has become worn and can no longer serve us, we do not cry because it has gone the way of all jackets; we simply take it off, hang it up carefully, and go home.

Perhaps it would not be out of place here to mention reincarnation, as it is interpreted in Eastern mysticism. The Hindu and Buddhist scriptures tell us that when consciousness is consolidated at the moment of death, our last thought will sum up our life. At that instant, all the desires of our lifetime are consolidated in one deep, driving desire, which sums up our destiny. It is this desire which impels us to take a body again, so that these desires may be satisfied.

According to this presentation, we are reborn into a context that is ideally suited for us to work on our weak points. If our last thoughts are of ourselves, we will be reborn into a family and environment just right for showing us that by living for ourselves we can never find fulfillment. But if we have learned to live not for ourselves but for others, and our last thought is not of ourselves but of the Lord, then when we die we no longer have any personal desires to fulfill, and we merge quietly and peacefully into the Lord. We have already been united with him in our lifetime, and when it falls away, the body no more disturbs this unity than a falling leaf disturbs the tree.

The mystics of Hinduism and Buddhism have a very expressive way of presenting this. They tell us that this world is like an immense school, where we have all been enrolled in order to learn that all life is one. This is the supreme goal of life, and our only reason for being here on earth is to discover this unity for ourselves. When we do this, the Lord says, "Very good; you've graduated. Now you don't have to go to school any more." But if at the end of our life we still have not made this discovery, the Lord tells us very compassionately, "I think you'd better come back next semester and work a little harder."

I have heard that W. C. Fields wanted his epitaph

to read, "On the whole, I'd rather be in Philadelphia." If that *was* his last wish, he may well be there now, disguised as someone else. In other words, whatever context we find ourselves in in this life, this is a choice which we have made ourselves. And the very positive aspect of this concept of reincarnation is that it places the responsibility for our spiritual evolution squarely on our own shoulders. We cannot complain that our society has molded us, that our parents have influenced us, and then sit back and say, "There is nothing I can do to change myself." There is everything that we can do. We got ourselves into the situation we are in, and we can get ourselves out once we begin to make the right choices in life.

In this way of looking at things, none of us is lost. We are all working towards the discovery of the unity of life, however long it may take. Our present life is a fresh opportunity to move closer to the supreme goal, and the choice is entirely ours whether we make the best use of this opportunity. This is a very practical, positive conclusion, and in fact reincarnation does such a good job of explaining the human condition that it is very difficult to question it, even intellectually. But I always emphasize that when it comes to making wise choices in life, it makes not the slightest difference whether we believe in reincarnation or not. No matter how many lives we believe in, death poses the same challenge to us all. It is possible to believe in a thousand lifetimes and still lead a selfish life, and it is possible to believe in only one lifetime and still learn to become established in the mantram and realize for ourselves the supreme goal of life.

Whether or not we believe in reincarnation, whether or not we even believe that life has a goal, the mantram can be of enormous value at the hour of death. We do not need to repeat it for years to draw upon its power at such a critical time. Any remembrance of the Holy Name is a solace that can help us to undergo the last great change called death with peace and courage in our hearts.

The Goal of Life ❧

Twenty-five hundred years ago, ordinary people like you and me used to gather around the Compassionate Buddha, dazzled by the radiance of his personality, and ask, "Are you a god? Are you an angel?" The Buddha would answer quietly, "No, I am awake." This is the literal meaning of the word *buddha,* "he who has awakened"—awakened from the nightmare of separate living into the light of unity.

This awakening is the highest goal of life, and though different religions call it by different names, the goal is one and the same. It is nirvana to the Buddhist, moksha to the Hindu; Jesus the Christ calls it beautifully "entering the kingdom of heaven within." To the Sufis it is union with the Beloved; to Jewish mystics it is the return to the Promised Land. Sometimes it is called Christ-consciousness or Krishna-consciousness, enlightenment, illumination, or Self-realization. But there is no difference between any of these, as we can see when we keep our eyes on the goal

191

itself rather than on the innumerable differences in rites and rituals and dogmas. No matter what they call it, all the great religions point to the same supreme goal.

Every one of us has an aching need for a goal worthy of our complete dedication, for an ideal so lofty that we can keep our eyes on it no matter what circumstances come our way. Much of our boredom and restlessness comes from not having a direction in life; we are like someone all dressed up on a Saturday night with nowhere to go. If I may say so, most of what we call goals are not real goals at all, because they give us no all-encompassing sense of purpose in life. But when we have an overriding goal, we find that many of our problems fall away of their own accord. Everything falls into perspective: we know what to do with our time, what to do with our energy, and it is easier to see all the little choices that confront us every day. Shall I eat what appeals to the taste buds, or what conduces to sound health? Shall I spend time doing my own thing, or doing work which benefits all those around me? Shall I move away from people just because their ways are not my ways, or shall I try to live in harmony with everyone around me? When we have our eyes on the goal of life we see these choices everywhere, all the time, and we begin to cultivate the will and wisdom to make the choices which will help us to grow to our full stature. Thus we gradually wake up to our true nature, which is ever pure, ever perfect.

At present, however, most of us are far from having this supreme goal always in sight. The vast majority of us are obsessively identified with our body, our emotions, our intellect, and our ego. We have come to believe that we are separate individuals whose fulfillment lies in seeking our own satisfaction, even at the expense of those around us.

In traditional circles we hear a good deal about heaven and hell, and many people say they do not believe in them. But heaven and hell are not places; they are states of consciousness. Hell is not a bit of over-heated subterranean real estate where devils dance about with pitchforks; it is what we experience whenever we are plagued by worry or anger or jealousy or greed. Hell is the increasing loneliness and frustration we feel when we try to live for ourselves as separate individuals. And heaven, too, is a state of consciousness, which we can all enjoy right in this very life when we no longer see ourselves as separate. When we overcome our identification with the body, the mind, and the ego, we are living in freedom. When we come to see that our fulfillment lies in making the greatest possible contribution to our family, our society, and our world, we are living in harmony with the unity of life. This is living in joy; this is heaven here and now.

In the Judeo-Christian tradition, the monstrous superstition that we are all separate is symbolized by the Fall; in the Hindu and Buddhist tradition it is called *maya*. *Maya* is a term we often hear now in the West, where it is usually translated as illusion. Literally, however, *maya* means "that which can be measured." Maya is the finite world which we perceive with the senses and grasp with the intellect; it is the world of change that is subject to death and decay. When we identify with the body, mind, and ego, with the set of habits that we are pleased to call our personality, we are wrongly identifying with maya. And as long as we are under the hypnotic spell of maya—which I like to think is connected with the word *magic*—we will go on believing that we can find lasting fulfillment in sensory pleasures, in amassing money, in acquiring great learning, in imposing our self-will on those around us.

But whatever temporary satisfaction these pursuits may give us, they cannot bring us the abiding joy that we are all seeking. Saint Augustine brings this point home when he cries out: "Lord, how can I ever find rest anywhere else when I am made to rest in thee?" What we are all looking for, even though we may be searching in the most improbable places, is infinite wisdom, infinite joy, infinite love—in other words, the Lord. And this is our real nature. At the very core of our being is a spark of purity, of perfection, of divinity, because the Lord is enshrined in the heart of each of us. When we learn to identify less and less with that which is subject to change and more and more with this core of perfection, we are gradually waking up to our true nature.

This awakening, as the Compassionate Buddha would say, is something each of us must do for himself or herself. When people would come to the Buddha and say, "Blessed One, please tell us all about this nirvana that you speak of," he would smile and reply, "Learn to meditate, so that you may find out for yourself." In other words, realizing the unity of life is not an intellectual understanding; it is an experiential discovery. It is impossible to convey in words what awareness of the unity of life is like, what it is like to have attained the highest goal that life has to offer. Shankara, the great mystic from my old state of Kerala, tells us that words and thoughts turn back frightened when they try to approach the ultimate Reality. It is not measurable, so how can thoughts grasp it or words define it? Even the most inspired mystics, in the most inspired language, can only hint at it; they use words to pique our curiosity and to rouse our enthusiasm to have this experience ourselves. As Sri Ramakrishna tells us, when you have eaten a mango, you know what mangoes taste like; if you have not, the description will not mean much unless you resolve to go out and taste one for yourself.

But although the ultimate Reality cannot be grasped by words or thoughts, the great mystics often go on to tell us what realization of this goal means in practical terms, what effect it has on daily living. Realization is experiential; it has a profound impact on our conduct, character, and consciousness. In the homely language of Sri Ramakrishna, when a man has eaten garlic, every breath that comes out of him will smell of garlic. When a man or woman has realized the indivisible unity of life, then everything he does, every word she utters, will be an expression of this unity. This is the infallible test of spiritual experience. You may have a bumper sticker that says All Life Is One, but if you do not have some measure of control over your thinking process, if you cannot drop a job at will or juggle with your likes and dislikes, if you cannot bear patiently with those who oppose you, then you have not yet realized the unity of life for yourself.

People usually smile and nod in approval when I say that we can come to identify more and more with the spark of divinity in all of us. But when I say that we must identify less with the body, the mind, and the ego, they begin to shift uneasily in their seats, and when I mention detachment, which is absolutely necessary for attaining the goal of life, they sometimes get up and tiptoe out the back door. The word *detachment* often strikes a negative note, but detachment is really a marvelous quality; it is the key to intentional living. Detachment does not mean that we are indifferent or unconcerned, but that we are not entangled. Detachment from work, for instance, doesn't mean that we lean back with our feet up on our desk. We work harder than ever; we do our very best, but we are not caught in the results. We don't worry about the job, and we don't get elated if we get the results we wanted or depressed if we do not. If I may say so, it is the detached worker who does the best job. Such people can put their work in a larger perspective and do it with objectivity and concentration. And in personal relations, detachment is invaluable. Only when we are detached can we really see the needs of the other person; we can respect his opinions and not get agitated by his shortcomings.

When we cease to identify ourselves with the body, we come to see it for what it is: a very useful instrument of service. As my Grandmother used to tell me, "Son, the Lord gave you these two hands not to strike at others, but to wipe away their tears." We use the body wisely like any other tool; in fact, I am fond of comparing the body to a compact car. We take good care of it by keeping it clean and giving it nourishing food in temperate quantities, and we keep it in good running order by giving it plenty of exercise. But we should never forget that we are the driver; our senses should obey us just the way well-trained horses respond to the slightest touch on the reins. When the palate clamors for something sweet but not very healthy, we should be able to say, "That's not so good for you," and the palate should reply, "Yes, boss; I won't ask again."

When we have lost our identification with the body, we no longer identify others with their bodies, either. This means that we will not try to base a relationship just on physical appeal, and we will be incapable of discriminating against others on the basis of race or color. Loss of body-consciousness does not mean that we go around bumping into things, but that we no longer try to base our security on the body. This gives us a good deal of immunity to disease, especially psychosomatic ailments; it gives us abundant vitality throughout our life and leaves us unperturbed by the ravages of time on the body.

When we cease to identify ourselves with the mind, we come to see it, too, as a very useful instrument. It is our internal instrument, just as the body is the external instrument. The mind is adept at pulling things apart, looking for cause and effect, labeling and classifying. I am not deprecating the well-trained intellect; it is quite useful in solving certain kinds of problems, such as how to get water from the well to the house or how to land a man on the moon. But intellectual knowledge alone will not get us very far in life. You may know all about quantum physics, but this is of very little use when you are in emotional turmoil. You may have written an article on the word *forgiveness* in the New Testament, but can you remain unagitated when someone criticizes your article? Sri Ramakrishna calls intellectual knowledge "rice and banana knowledge": it is useful for buying our food, sometimes for getting things done, but it doesn't really help us to live. We must be able to put what we know into practice for the art of living.

When we do not identify ourselves with the mind, we keep our minds open and youthful. Our likes and dislikes are held lightly, and we can juggle with them just as a trained juggler juggles with those colored balls. We enjoy things we like; we enjoy things we used not to like if they benefit those around us; we can drop a job at will. We can throw a pet opinion out into the arena and let everybody trample on it while we look on in detached interest. If the opinion is damaged, we discard it; if it is still intact, we keep it, and often those who just danced on this very same opinion will say, "That is a good opinion; we would like to share it with you." And if a resentful thought happens to rise in our mind, we do not get all agitated and say, "I am resentful"; we just watch that little resentful thought sail out of sight into the distance. It is only when we identify with our thoughts and dwell on them that this stray wisp of resentfulness can billow up and cover the sky like a dark monsoon cloud. With increasing detachment from our thoughts, we find the mind becoming less and less subject to ups and downs, vacillations, and oscillations; our concentration improves, and we are able to accomplish a great deal of work without tension and without fatigue.

At last, when we cease to identify with the ego, we are no longer looking at life through our own needs and prejudices; we see life whole. At present, most of us see ourselves as a separate fragment in a world of fragments. We are looking at life through the little keyhole of our own ego, and of course our view is very narrow, very limited, very disoriented. We think of ourselves first; "look out for number one" is an apt motto for the ego. "How will this situation affect me?" the ego asks. "How can I manipulate that person to my benefit; how can I grab as much as I can and give as little as I can?"

People who identify strongly with the ego tend to have a great deal of self-will in their relations with other people. I am always reminded of this when I see those huge trailers on the freeway with the little red sign at the back: *Caution—Wide Load*. These vehicles take up all of their own lane and some of the lanes on either side too. On smaller roads, other vehicles can barely get by them, and oncoming cars practically have to drive into the ditch. People with a wide load of self-will go through life like this; they should have that little red sign at the back too: Wide Load. They are insensitive to the needs of others; they try to impose their self-will on those around them and shove other people out of the way without even realizing what they are doing. It is only natural in life that such people are disliked and avoided, and end up more and more lonely and insecure.

When we are locked into ourselves through compulsive identification with the ego, it is very much like being in prison. The greater our identification with the ego, the higher and stronger are the walls of our private Bastilles. When we see life whole, we are no longer looking at the world through that little keyhole; we have enlarged the keyhole, then removed the door, and finally even demolished the prison walls. Then we are naturally sensitive to other people's needs, other people's points of view. We are able to help them effectively, and we become incapable of blaming them or holding the past against them. We come to see that in exploiting others we are working to the detriment of all, and we can forgo our own satisfactions gladly if this will contribute to the welfare of our family, our friends, and our society. We come to see the joy of others as our joy and their suffering as our suffering, and we have the will and wisdom to help alleviate this suffering and contribute to their joy.

This, of course, is a complete change in our usual perspective. To see the whole we have to turn our back on the ego; to see the unity we have to turn our back on separateness. As we begin to change our perspective in this way and come to see the indivisible unity of life, we will be amazed to see that we had always been looking at life upside down. Sometimes the scriptures and great mystics of all religions resort to seemingly paradoxical language to put this point across. Jesus tells us, "He who would seek to find himself shall lose himself, and he who loses himself shall find himself"; the person who overcomes identification with the limited ego will find the source of abiding joy and limitless love which is our real nature. As Saint Paul exclaims after becoming united with Christ, "Not I, not I, but Christ liveth in me."

But we do not turn our back on the ego overnight. We do not go to bed one night as a feverish fragment of ego-consciousness and wake up the next morning in blissful awareness of unity. This is not something that can be done by taking a pill or attending a weekend seminar, by reading books or plugging ourselves into alpha wave machines. It takes years of sustained effort, and it is anything but easy. There is a good deal of pain in going against self-will. You may feel that you have got to do as the ego dictates or you will die, and in a sense this is just what is happening. Each time you go against self-will, in little ways like remembering the needs of your family before your own or not postponing a disagreeable job, the ego shrinks just a little; the barrier between you and the Lord falls just a little. This is what the mystics call dying to self. Over a long, long time the separate ego dies completely, and we come to life in the Lord; we realize our unity with Him who is enshrined in the very depths of our consciousness. In the words of Meister Eckhart, a great German mystic, "The old man dies and the new man is born; the pauper dies and the prince is born."

When we are full of ourselves, we leave the Lord no room to enter our lives, but as we gradually empty ourselves of all that is selfish and separate in us, the Lord can fill us with himself. In the Hindu tradition, there is a story in which the Lord, represented as Sri Krishna, was playing on his flute while Radha, who stands for the human soul longing for union with the divine, watched with her eyes full of envy. "What has your flute done to enjoy the blessing of being held up to your lips hour after hour?" she asked. Sri Krishna took the flute from his lips and held it so that Radha could see inside. "Look, it's completely empty," he said, "so I can fill it with my divine melody."

The Bhagavad Gita tells us that we have only one enemy in the world: our will, and only one friend in the world: our will. When we let self-will propel us to seek our own private satisfactions at the expense of those around us, then our will really is our own worst enemy, because it is alienating us from the source of abiding joy and unshakable security within us. On the other hand, when we turn our will against the ego, taking advantage of the innumerable little opportunities throughout the day to reduce self-will, then the will is helping us to grow to our full stature.

For the vast majority of us, our will is operative only on the surface level of consciousness. We have no say in what goes on deeper in consciousness, where most of our problems have their roots. But we can learn to deepen our will, to strengthen it immeasurably. You must have seen weight-lifters showing off their biceps on Muscle Beach—in my mother tongue we call this "making frogs leap under the skin." Strengthening the will is very much like developing our muscles: an unused will atrophies, and a will that is exercised regularly grows. When Jesus teaches us to pray, "Thy will be done," he is reminding us that in exercising our will to overcome our separateness and selfishness, we are remaking ourselves into instruments of the divine will.

Meister Eckhart tells us in vivid language why sustained effort is necessary to effect this transformation. He says that we all have the seed of God within us, just as pears have pear seeds and apples have apple seeds. But the wise gardener doesn't expect a tree laden with ripe apples to appear by magic. He plants the seed in the proper soil, waters it and weeds around it, and then protects the young tree for many years and prunes it carefully, so that it will bear good fruit. Similarly, the God-seed is waiting to germinate in the depths of our consciousness, but we must all cultivate our potential for spiritual awareness by sustained and systematic effort. And as Gandhi tells us, full effort is full victory.

Yet, though we must put forth all our effort, I have no hesitation in saying that ultimately it is the grace of the Lord that sets us free. We have to practice meditation regularly and systematically, repeat the mantram at every opportunity, and make every effort to reduce our self-will by observing all the other spiritual disciplines too, but we cannot attain the goal by human effort alone. From any genuine mystic in any religious tradition, you will hear the same note of awe and wonder: how did I, so weak, so full of shortcomings, succeed in overcoming all these immense obstacles?

In the early days, grace may come to us as the

desire to overcome desire—the desire to have some mastery over our thinking process. For a long time in life we take it for granted that we must be buffeted about by self-centered desires and cravings, at the mercy of the senses and the mind. But finally we get tired of being buffeted about, and it slowly dawns on us that we could have some say in what goes on in consciousness. One of my friends tells me that he was once walking along just after turning in a term paper that he had been working on for days. "I'm a free man now," he said, but all sorts of miscellaneous thoughts about things he ought to have put into the paper kept tumbling through his mind. "I don't have to stand for this," he thought, and it occurred to him to repeat *Om* in the back of his mind. He didn't know exactly what *Om* meant, but he had heard of it as a sacred formula, and it seemed better to repeat that than to keep thinking about a paper that had already been turned in. That, of course, is exactly what the mantram is for, and it laid to rest all those other thoughts that had been nagging him. This is the rising desire to have some control over consciousness, and a few months later this friend took to the practice of meditation after hearing me present the spiritual life as the path that leads to freedom.

The desire to go beyond desire is the longing for freedom rising from deep within us. In the language of Sri Ramakrishna, the Divine Mother has looked upon us from the corner of her beautiful eyes, filled with love for us. When that glance falls on us, there comes the desire to be free, and the will to practice the disciplines which will set us free.

Grace may come to us in many unsuspected forms in the early days. For some it comes as a deep restlessness, which arises from being dissatisfied with living life on the surface level of consciousness. Often this shows up as dissatisfaction with our old pursuits, or the quality of our living or our personal relationships, or even with ourselves. Many times people have confessed to me, "I just don't like myself," and I take this as a very promising sign. Why should we be satisfied with ourselves as we are now, when we have vastly greater reserves of strength and wisdom within us?

At first we may try to relieve this restlessness by switching jobs, or changing life styles, or traveling to distant places. Eventually, however, we see that nothing can satisfy us except turning inwards and mastering ourselves. If any of this kind of dissatisfaction leads us to turn inwards and take up the practice of the spiritual life, that is a sure sign of grace.

Often restlessness drives us into all sorts of adventures, in which we keep seeking new challenges to pit ourselves against. No sooner have we met one challenge than we need a bigger one. This is what motivates many mountain climbers, for example. Climbing is arduous and dangerous, and the challenge and the concentration and commitment it requires change all its hardships into joy. So even looking for adventure may be the call from within. In setting out to cross the sea of the mind, you will find a lifelong challenge which will test every ounce of your endurance.

In the early days, when grace first touches us, we often don't understand it; we may even struggle against it. As we become more and more restless, more and more dissatisfied with life on the surface level of consciousness, we may throw ourselves even more recklessly into the pursuit of pleasure or profit. As Meister Eckhart puts it, we thrash about like a fish caught by the divine fisherman's hook. The hook has entered the fish's flesh, and as it struggles to get free, the hook only goes in deeper and deeper. We fling ourselves with redoubled zeal into our old pursuits, hoping to get the same old satisfaction from them; but the more we try, the less satisfaction we find and the more frustrated we become. Only after a long time does it finally dawn on us that we may be beginning to get free. This is the touch of divine grace.

But grace is not a matter of letting the Lord do all the work for us. In order to make progress on the spiritual path, we need to have the grace of our own mind as well. We need to strengthen our will and make the wise choices which will lead us closer to realizing the indivisible unity of life. In the early years, it is very much as if we are doing all the work ourselves; only near the end of the journey can we look back and see that even our own effort has been an expression of grace. A great Sufi mystic tells us that once, in a moment of despair, he cried out with all his heart: "Allah, Allah, how long I've been calling on you, and you still have not revealed yourself to me!" In the depths of his consciousness he heard the voice of God reply, "Who do you think has been making you call on me all this time?"

The Mantram & Other Spiritual Disciplines ❧

Once, the story goes, there was a sculptor in India who was famous for his statues of elephants, which were so perfect in every detail that to see one you would expect it to raise its trunk and trumpet. "How do you manage to carve such lifelike elephants?" people would ask. "It's very simple," the sculptor would reply. "I just find a big rock, take a hammer and some chisels, and remove everything that is not elephant."

In just the same way, you and I can make ourselves perfect by removing from our consciousness every trace of separateness and selfishness. What is left is our real Self, which is divine. I have deep appreciation for great music, great literature, and great art, but each of these expresses only one small facet of our selves. To me, it appeals much more deeply to make our whole life a work of art, our every word and deed an expression of the unity of life. This is the highest art there is, and all the world's great religions have given us the tools we need to practice it, in a comprehensive body of spiritual disciplines of which the mantram is only one.

In different traditions, these disciplines are called by different names and expressed in different words—the Buddha's Noble Eightfold Path, medieval Catholicism's Seven Gifts of the Holy Spirit—but they are all intended to lead us to the same goal. These disciplines are timeless; they are as relevant to the human condition now as they were in India twenty-five hundred years ago or on the shores of Galilee in Jesus' time. They are undertaken not for the sake of discipline itself or because the scriptures say to, but because men and women of God everywhere have verified in their own lives that these disciplines can lead us to the supreme goal of life, which is the realization that all life is one.

This is not rhetoric. Realizing the unity of life is an experiential discovery that we can make for ourselves if we are prepared to make the effort required. But this is not something to be undertaken lightly or without guidance. Just as we would not set out to climb a mountain without first getting maps and finding an experienced guide who knows every foot of the ascent, we need an experienced spiritual teacher if we want to go to the summit of human consciousness. I have no hesitation in saying that this realization is impossible without the close guidance of a man or woman who has already discovered the unity of life in his or her own consciousness. Such a person cautions us against pitfalls and blind alleys along the way, encourages us as the challenges become greater, and inspires us by his or her personal example when we lose faith. But while the teacher is essential for guidance and support, we have to do the work for ourselves. Spiritual awareness is not something that just strikes us one day, like the apple falling on Sir Isaac Newton's head, and there is no shortcut to it such as taking drugs or using alpha wave gadgets. It must be cultivated by the hard work of eliminating all that is selfish and separate in us, following a body of disciplines that is based on our teacher's own personal experience in realizing the unity of life.

On the strength of my own small experience, let me present a comprehensive eightfold body of spiritual disciplines which I have found extremely useful. These disciplines are suited for life in the modern world, and they can be practiced by any man or woman capable of some resolution, some endurance, and some sense of dedication. They do not require you to withdraw into a cave and roll a rock across the entrance behind you; you can follow this program while living in the world among family and friends, while studying on the campus or working at a job. If I may pay a loving tribute to my own spiritual teacher, my mother's mother, this is her real genius. I have great respect for the monastic tradition, but to lead the spiritual life, my Grandmother taught me, we don't have to retire from life; we don't have to leave our family, drop out of school, or give up our job. I am irresistibly drawn to the artistry of this approach, in which we live in the midst of the world but never take our eyes off the supreme goal of life.

1. Meditation

Meditation comes first among spiritual disciplines. It is not a religion; it is a technique which enables us to realize for ourselves the unity of life within any of the world's great religious traditions, or even if we profess no religion at all. There is a popular misconception that meditation is making your mind a blank, or wool-gathering, or letting your mind wander around some theme. Meditation is anything but these; it is a dynamic discipline in concentration which enables us to unify our consciousness completely.

Most of us live on the surface level of conscious-ness, our grasshopper minds jumping from one subject to another, one desire to another, one distraction to another. But as the mind is concentrated in meditation, we learn to extend our conscious control over succes-sively deeper realms of consciousness, just as a diver learns to take deeper and deeper dives until he is able to walk about on the seabed. In the climax of meditation, on the seabed of consciousness, we realize that we are not limited by the confines of the body or mind or even of the ego; we discover for ourselves the source of abiding joy and infinite love that is our real nature.

For your meditation, memorize an inspirational passage from the scriptures and mystical literature of the world's great religions—for example, the Prayer of Saint Francis of Assisi, or the Twenty-third Psalm, or the last nineteen verses in the second chapter of the Bhagavad Gita. Choose passages which are simple and positive, and which bear the imprint of a great mystic's own personal experience. If you have memorized a number of such passages, that will help to avoid the possibility of the passage becoming stale or mechanical. Then, with your eyes gently closed, go through the words of the passage in your mind as slowly as you can. Do not follow any association of ideas, but keep to the words of the passage. When distractions come, do not resist them, but give more and more of your attention to the words of the passage. The secret here is that we become what we meditate on; sustained concentration on the inspirational passage drives it deep into our consciousness.

Meditation is a perfect way to begin the day. It is good to have your meditation as early as is convenient for you, while the morning is still and cool and before the noise and bustle of the day begins. Devote half an hour each morning to the practice of meditation; do not increase this half-hour period, but if you want to meditate more, have half an hour in the evening also. In addition to a fixed time, it is also good to have a fixed place for meditation—if not a room, at least a special corner. It should be quiet, cool, clean, and well ventilated. Keep that room for meditation, the repetition of the mantram, and spiritual reading only; do not use it for any other purpose. Gradually it will become so closely associated with meditation for you that you will have only to go into that room to become a little more calm, a little more patient, a little more loving.

You may sit on the floor for your meditation or in a straight-back chair, preferably one with arms. It is not important whether you sit in the full lotus position or the half lotus or in no lotus at all; the important thing about posture is that you sit with your head, neck, and spinal column in a straight line and your eyes gently closed. As your concentration deepens, your nervous system will begin to relax and you may experience drowsiness. When this happens, draw yourself up and move away from your back support.

Under no circumstances should you skip your meditation. If necessary, get up a little earlier to be sure that you have enough time. There is a saying in India that if you skip one day's meditation, it takes seven days to catch up. A fixed time and a fixed place are a great aid to regularity in meditation, which when practiced with regularity and sustained enthusiasm can bring about a marvelous transformation of consciousness.

Very often when people think of someone seated motionless in meditation with eyes closed, they say, "Meditation is passive; meditation is turning in on yourself." Let me assure you that meditation is anything but passive. It is hard, hard work, even though the work is all being done on the inside. But the will and concentration we develop in meditation are meant to be turned outwards, to be applied in our work, in our studies, in our relations with other people. It is very much like an athlete doing the broad jump. When he goes back to get a running start, the spectators don't say, "Look, he's going in the wrong direction; he's not going to jump!" They know that he is going back to get the distance he needs for a good running start, which will carry him much further than if he had just jumped from where he stood. When we turn inward in meditation, we are getting the momentum we need to leap far in our daily life. As our meditation improves, we learn to jump right over our petty likes and dislikes to do our work with concentration and detachment, passing through personal relations with graceful artistry and a minimum of friction.

2. Repetition of the Mantram

Next to meditation, repetition of the mantram is perhaps the most powerful of spiritual techniques when practiced as part of a comprehensive approach to spiritual living. Meditation is a discipline which requires sustained effort and will; the mantram requires neither to be effective. I like to say that repeating the mantram is like calling the Lord collect. You call the Lord and say "I don't have any money, so don't send me any bills; I don't have any will, so don't ask me to undergo any disciplines," and the Lord replies with infinite patience, "Never mind; I'll pay the bill. It's enough that you even thought of me at all."

In most orthodox Hindu traditions and even by some mystics of the Roman Catholic and Eastern Orthodox churches in the West, the mantram itself is used for meditation. This is sometimes confusing to those who are following the eightfold path presented here, so I find it helpful to draw a sharp distinction between meditation and the repetition of the mantram. Meditation is a rigorous discipline, for which I have found a long inspirational passage to be most effective in our modern, intellectually oriented age. But the mantram requires no discipline; you may repeat it at virtually any time and in any place. If your mind wanders from the mantram, if you forget it altogether, there is no cause for regret. But the more often you remember the mantram, particularly in situations where you need to strengthen your will, the deeper it will sink into your consciousness and the greater will be the benefit you derive from repeating it.

3. Slowing Down

Slowing down is a great aid to efficiency, to concentration, and to physical and emotional health. The quality of life suffers when we live under the constant pressure of time, always watching the clock and trying to make every second count. The person who can do a job fastest is not necessarily the one who can do it best. All too often when we hurry we do a shoddy job, or make mistakes which take longer to correct than if we had been slow and careful in the first place. And it is difficult to give a job our full attention when we are in a hurry. Hurry means tension and a host of physical problems which come in its wake. And hurry makes for superficial relationships, because it deprives our family and friends of our time and attention so that we are not able to be sensitive to their needs.

When I first came to this country, well-meaning friends told me, "You will be terribly shocked by the pace of life, but gradually you will adapt to it." I am happy to say that I have *not* adapted to it—not only that, but I have succeeded in slowing down a good many of my friends. But I am still grieved by the frantic pace I see around me every day. Recently I went to a coffee shop with a few friends, and I was amazed by the speed of both customers and waitresses. As we were going in, we saw a couple hurrying in with a little girl by the hand. They were in a rush to get their coffee and had forgotten that little children have short legs and take little steps, so they were dragging her along so fast that the girl fell and skinned her knee. Inside, no sooner had we been seated than we heard a plate crashing to the floor. The waitress who took our order didn't even seem to see us, and when she banged the cups down in front of us, she was gone before we could even say thank you. Far from blaming this woman, who was under a great deal of pressure, I had great sympathy for her. I would not be surprised if anyone who eats at that place gets indigestion, or if anyone who works there for long develops an ulcer; this is what hurry and pressure do to us.

In order to slow down, it is a great help to begin the day early. Get up in plenty of time for meditation, if you meditate, and for a leisurely breakfast with your family or friends. The pace with which you begin the day is the pace you will maintain throughout the day. If you find yourself getting speeded up, repeat the mantram as a reminder to slow down. Don't try to schedule your time too rigidly, or you will only find yourself getting harried and frustrated as you inevitably fall behind schedule. It may help to eliminate some unnecessary activities from your day, if they are not part of your legitimate responsibility to family or study or work or if they do not contribute to your spiritual growth.

Your personal example of unhurried concentration will not only help you; it will help those around you, too. I remember once at Christmastime waiting in a long line at the post office. I waited quietly, repeating the mantram, while the man behind me was breathing fire and brimstone down my neck—he was probably double-parked outside. After a while I turned to him and said, "I am in no hurry; why don't you take my place?" The poor chap muttered something about being caught in the rat race and relaxed visibly. The girl at the window was new at the job; she was a student working during the Christmas vacation, and she was getting more and more rattled as people pressured her to weigh their packages and give them their change faster and faster. So to her, too, I said, "You take your time; I am in no hurry." It helped her greatly. But we don't have to tell people that we are not in a hurry; we communicate it through our example of patience, concentration, and consideration for others, and everyone around us benefits.

4. One-pointedness

One-pointed concentration is the mark of the person who is able to make a real contribution to any field he studies, to any task she tries her hand at. But in the modern world we have become so accustomed to dividing our attention that we take it for granted: we eat popcorn while watching a movie, we smoke while reading the paper, and we listen to music while we work or study. On the Berkeley campus, I have seen students in the cafeteria reading the *Daily Californian* with one eye and watching passers-by with the other, while listening to background music, drinking a cup of coffee, and smoking a cigarette, all at the same time. Their attention is scattered in five directions.

When we divide our attention this way, we cannot do full justice to any of the things we are attending to: we do not really taste the popcorn, and we do not really see the whole movie, either. I would say that anything that is worth doing is worth giving our full attention to. Just as sunlight concentrated by a magnifying glass is able to set paper afire, one-pointed concentration on your work or studies will improve efficiency, eliminate tension, and banish boredom. And one-pointedness during the day is a tremendous aid to concentration in any field, on any subject.

When we are able to give our one-pointed attention to everything we do, other people cannot help responding deeply, no matter what the relationship: man and woman, parent and child, teacher and student, friend and friend. When we are talking to someone, for example, we should be able to give our full attention to the person we are talking to. If we look only at him, listen only to her, and do not think of what we will say in reply or how we can change the subject, we will not only improve our own concentration but benefit the other person as well. I like to tell my friends that if Romeo is talking to Juliet, he should not take his eyes off her even if an elephant walks into the room. Children particularly thrive on this sort of attention. They are very keen observers, and they know when we are not really there. By giving them our full attention, we assure them of our love far more than when we buy them toys or send them off to the movies for the afternoon, and we are doing them a great service by setting a personal example of one-pointedness.

5. Training the Senses

Whenever I talk about sense restraint, I make a point of emphasizing that I do not mean denial of the senses, but discriminating restraint—with the accent on "discriminating." We could also call it training the senses; it is the same. Most of us have never trained our senses to obey us; we have senses like unruly pups, yapping all night, biting our hand with their sharp little teeth, and chewing up our favorite shoes. In the case of a really big sense craving, it is more like a huge Great Dane dragging us along at the end of a leash. Indulging the senses weakens our will, makes our mind more restless, increases our identification with the body, and leaves us a prey to a host of physical ailments. I am not moralizing or being puritanical when I say this; I am being practical. It grieves me to see people smoking, drinking, overeating, not getting exercise, or keeping late hours, because I know that they are injuring themselves. So sense restraint is not a grim form of self-torture; it leads to sound health, greater security, and a sense of freedom.

There is a good deal of artistry in training the senses, too. The time to leave the dinner table, for instance, is not after you have eaten one piece of pie too many, but just when everything still tastes delicious and you would like to have just a little bit more. You stop of your own free will. There is a real sense of mastery in this, and an artistry that is absent in staying on at the table until you can scarcely move and a vague sense of regret has set in.

In other words, training the senses plays an invaluable role in learning to live in freedom. Mahatma Gandhi tells us on the basis of his own experience that control of the palate is an invaluable aid to control of the mind. If we can learn to go beyond our likes and dislikes in food and eat nourishing food in temperate quantities only when we are hungry, then we will have taken a big step towards keeping our mind even.

All the senses are pathways into consciousness. In Sanskrit, one of the words for eating means not only eating through the mouth but eating through all the senses. We eat ice cream through the mouth; we eat television through the eyes and ears. It all goes in and becomes part of consciousness. When people sit with their eyes glued to the screen during some sensate movie, they are having a seven-course meal. It never occurs to most of us that we could have some say over what goes into our consciousness. At present, anything can go in; we have no doorkeepers; the doors are open all the time. But we can learn to stop what goes in and check its credentials at the door: "This show will agitate me and give me nightmares, so I'm not going to let it come in; that book will make me more patient, so I will let it come in." There are choices to make every day in what we eat, what books we read, what kind of television we watch, what sort of conversations we have. It is by making wise choices in all these little matters that we become healthy, happy, secure, selfless, and beautiful; and one of the best ways to remind ourselves of this choice is to say the mantram.

6. Putting Others First

When we remember the needs of others and put their welfare before our own, we are gradually breaking out of the prison of our own separateness. When we go only after what pleases us and try to impose our self-will on those around us, we are building the walls of the ego-prison even higher. One of the reasons I put so much stress on the family is that it gives us countless opportunities throughout the day for reducing our self-will by putting others first. This is often extremely difficult in emotionally entangled relationships. Even if you have a headache and you're in a bad mood, it's not too hard to smile at the bank teller or say thank you to the sales clerk, but just see what happens when you get home. All too often we take out our irritability and frustration on those closest to us. This is the time to cultivate more patience, to stop dwelling on ourselves and think more of the needs of others. Above all, we should learn to cooperate rather than to compete—particularly in the home between man and woman, where competition pulls the family asunder. None of this need be done on a grand scale, with the whole world watching; it can be done in many little ways as we become more sensitive to the needs of others.

Putting other people first is showing your love for them, but this love expresses itself in different ways. In putting the postman first, for instance, you don't run out and throw your arms around him and tell him how wonderful he is; you put him first by addressing your letters neatly and legibly and by being sure to include the zip code. You put your children first by giving them as much of your time and attention as possible, by respecting their point of view, and by remembering always to set the sort of personal example that you would like them to follow. After all, it won't have much effect when you shake your finger at your son or daughter and say "I don't want you to drink" if you have a cocktail glass in the other hand. You are also putting your children first if you help them not to develop too much self-will or to get too caught up in likes and dislikes; this kind of freedom is much more easily learned when we are young, and it will save them a great deal of unnecessary suffering.

If we really want to make progress on the spiritual path, there is no substitute for putting others first. It is the give-and-take of innumerable little encounters with others in our daily life that really wears off the angles and corners of the ego. Unless we reduce our self-will like this, we will simply have too wide a load of self-will to get through some of the strait and narrow gates into our deeper consciousness.

This is why I repeat everywhere that the spiritual life is best led in the midst of people. If we leave our family, give up our job, or drop out of school to go live in a cave high on the Himalayas, three days' journey from the nearest human being, we may find a certain peace of mind, but this is not the kind of peace that lasts. The trees won't offend us; the squirrels won't contradict us; our self-will will play dead because there is no one to rouse it, and we may say, "Ah, how calm and spiritual I am!" But when we come back into the midst of life, dealing with people whose ways are not our ways, we will be more agitated than ever. So let me assure you that whatever your present situation is, it is an excellent one for taking up the spiritual life.

Someone once asked me in very graphic language if putting the other person first all the time doesn't mean making yourself into a doormat. Not at all. We are not really putting others first if we connive at their mistakes, or if we let them have their way when they want to go in some wrong direction. It is a sign of great love and great maturity to be able to oppose the other person tenderly and resolutely when he or she is going in the wrong direction. When it seems necessary to say no, we should be able to say it gently and without the slightest trace of resentment or retaliation. We can all learn to disagree without being disagreeable.

7. Readings in Mysticism

Readings in the scriptures and the great mystics of all religions can be a great source of inspiration on the spiritual path. If you want to know more about mysticism and the real goal of religion, do not go to books about mysticism or religion; go direct to the great mystics themselves. They have left us a rich heritage of practical commentary on the scriptures, beautiful poetry, and the inspiring stories of their own personal discovery of the unity of life. These writings are meant to be read slowly and thoughtfully, a few pages at a time, so that you can reflect over what you read. It is particularly helpful to spend fifteen minutes or so in this kind of reading just before bedtime.

8. Association with Like-minded People

We all need companionship and support when we are changing the very basis of our life. It is difficult to practice meditation and undo all our old conditioning, and here association with spiritually oriented people is a source of day-to-day support and inspiration. In your own home, it is very good if members of the family meditate together, but friends, too, can live together and base their lives on the same spiritual values. If possible, it is of especially great value to meet and draw inspiration from someone who is able to interpret the sacred scriptures and the great mystics in the light of his or her own personal experience.

I have sometimes heard people ask whether practicing these disciplines isn't trying to buy the Lord's love, to make a bargain with the Lord. The Lord does not love us because we deserve it or because we have worked for it, but because his very nature is pure love. His love for us is infinite; it cannot be diminished or increased, but through the practice of meditation, repetition of the mantram, and observance of these other allied disciplines, we can make *our* love for him grow and deepen.

The Lord wants nothing more for each of us than that we should all be united with him. Even if, in our ignorance of this, we flounder around in life and cause suffering and confusion for ourselves and those around us, the only thing that will bring us real fulfillment is to realize in our own consciousness the indivisible unity of life. When we practice the disciplines on which the spiritual life is based, we reduce the suffering and confusion in our lives and make it easier for the Lord to draw us to him.

As Sri Ramakrishna said, the grace of God is a wind which is always blowing. All that you and I have to do is to put up our sails and let this wind carry us across the sea of life to the far shore, to the "peace that passeth all understanding." But most of us are firmly stuck on this shore. Our sail is in tatters and our boat cannot even move because of all the excess baggage weighing it down. It has taken us a lifetime to collect this baggage: all our likes and dislikes, our habits and opinions; all the resentments and hostilities which we have carefully nursed, all the things we are compulsively attached to. But through the systematic practice of spiritual disciplines, we gradually toss this excess baggage overboard, patch up our sail, and unfurl it to catch the wind that will carry us to the far shore. The wind is always blowing, but we have to do the work of making our boat seaworthy. This is why I seldom speak of divine grace to people. I talk about effort, because we have to put forth all our effort before grace will be forthcoming.

There is a saying in India that when we take one step toward the Lord, he takes seven steps toward us. The Lord is very eager to see us take the first step, but he knows us very well by now, and he watches carefully to see that we take that step and not wobble back and forth. It is not enough just to put your foot forward or even to touch it lightly to the ground; we must put our weight on it completely. When we do take a sincere step toward the Lord, by bearing patiently with those around us, or changing some unhealthy habits, or repeating the Holy Name, we can be sure that the Lord will take seven steps toward us. But we must take the first step.

The Interrelationship of Spiritual Disciplines

This body of spiritual disciplines that I recommend is a total way of life. It is not meant to be practiced just one day a week or only when we feel like it; it can be followed everywhere, throughout the day, in every aspect of daily life—in the home, on the campus, at work, and even in recreation. All these disciplines go together: when you work on one of them, it strengthens you in the others, and if you neglect one of them, it affects all of them adversely. Slowing down, for instance, helps in putting others first and in developing one-pointedness—which helps meditation, which in turn is an aid to remembering the mantram.

The disciplines of this eightfold path cover every aspect of our inner and outer life, our relationships with other people as well as our own physical and emotional well-being. By practicing all these disciplines together, we keep our inner and outer life in balance. Meditation is turning inwards, and it needs to be balanced with plenty of physical exercise, with work which demands our complete attention, and with association with other people. A good deal of energy is released in meditation, and there can sometimes be trouble if this energy is not harnessed during the rest of the day. As long as we are practicing the other disciplines sincerely too, we are sure to put this energy to good use.

As we enter deeper stages of consciousness in meditation, it is really like entering a jungle. We may come face to face with the tigers that prowl in the unconscious: an old fear, a deep-seated hostility, or a fierce compulsion. If we are practicing all the disciplines together, the timing works out very nicely: we will only develop the concentration necessary to get to the tiger's lair at the same time that we have the detachment and the will to fight it. This is why it is so dangerous to try shortcuts into the unconscious, like powerful drugs or occult breathing exercises; you can be catapulted right into the tiger's lair before you have any equipment to fight or protect yourself. In practical terms this can mean coming back to the surface level with a compulsion which will haunt you day and night, or perhaps getting trapped at a deeper level where you live in a dream world of your own. So these disciplines are meant to safeguard us, and I never recommend the practice of meditation without the allied disciplines.

In this eightfold program, the mantram plays a unique role as the bridge between the interior discipline of meditation and the other, external disciplines, for it helps greatly in applying the power gained in meditation to the other disciplines throughout the day. Meditation is like a big, broad-guage train with a powerful engine, which gradually lays down a track into the depths of our consciousness. The mantram travels this track like one of those handcars railway men use in India: two men push a lever back and forth a few times to get the handcar started; then, once it picks up speed, it rolls on effortlessly down the line. In railway work this handcar can be a very convenient way to get from one place to another, and in the same way we can use the mantram handcar to bring the resources we tap in meditation into play in our lives throughout the day. Then, when we find ourselves provoked or worried or driven by some compulsive habit, just remembering the mantram will enable us to recall a little of the inner strength we glimpsed that morning in meditation.

In this way, the mantram can give the day real continuity. At the beginning, it may only extend your morning meditation a little into breakfast. You may have felt at peace with the whole world in your meditation room, but when you sit down to burned toast and cold coffee, that is the end of your patience for the day. Gradually, however, as your meditation deepens and you try your best to remember the mantram at every possible moment, it will extend your morning meditation into your midmorning break, then to your lunch hour, and eventually into the afternoon. Finally, if you are practicing these disciplines sincerely, systematically, and with sustained enthusiasm, the mantram will enable you to take up your evening meditation exactly where you left off that morning. A lot of papers may have passed over your desk since your morning meditation; people may have interrupted you and irritated you and even spoken harshly to you; but if you have remembered the mantram whenever possible, none of these things will make a lasting impression on your mind. And if you make a similar effort to fall asleep in the mantram that night, it will be an unbroken thread throughout your sleep connecting your evening meditation with the next morning's. When this happens, it is a sure sign that you are beginning to make progress towards being established in the mantram permanently.

I must confess that in talking about all these spiritual disciplines, I have been unable to hide my partiality for meditation. But meditation is hard, hard work. It is a tremendous challenge, and in the latter stages of meditation, we are tested to the very limits of our endurance. I am not trying to scare anyone off; the truth is that many people, especially the young, respond enthusiastically to meditation all the more when I tell them how difficult it is and how much it demands. But of course there are many people who are not willing to make this kind of commitment. To such people I always hasten to add that the spiritual life is a come-as-you-are party; we all start from where we are. If you are not prepared to meditate, you can still benefit greatly from the practice of the other disciplines. Any step you take toward the Lord will bring you increased vitality, greater security, and richer relations with those around you. No matter what your background, you will benefit if you repeat the mantram at odd moments during the day or when you are walking or falling asleep, and you will benefit even more if the mantram enables you to slow down, to become more one-pointed, and to put others first.

Becoming Established
in the Mantram ✿

From the very first day you begin to use the mantram, it begins to grow in your consciousness. It germinates like the tiny seed that will eventually grow into a magnificent tree, and as you repeat it often and enthusiastically, it sends its roots deeper and deeper. Over a period of many years, if you have been practicing all the other spiritual disciplines which strengthen your will and deepen your concentration, the tap root of the mantram will extend fathoms deep, where it works to unify your consciousness—resolving old conflicts, solving problems you may not even be aware of, and transforming negative emotions into spiritual energy.

Finally, when this mantram root reaches the bedrock of consciousness, you become established in the mantram. It has become an integral part of your being, permeating your consciousness from the surface level down to the very depths. Then it is no longer necessary to repeat the mantram; it goes on repeating itself, echoing continuously at the very deepest levels of the mind. This is what Saint Paul means when he exhorts us to "pray without ceasing." As a Sufi mystic says, "Those who heard this word by the ear alone let it go out by the other ear; but those who heard it with their souls imprinted it on their souls and repeated it until it penetrated their hearts and souls, and their whole being became this word." In more homely language, it is as if after all these years of knocking—repeating the mantram assiduously whenever we get the chance— the mantram finally opens its doors and lets us in.

Becoming established in the mantram is one of the many marvelous developments which take place towards the very end of the spiritual journey, as we draw near to realizing the supreme goal of life. At this point, as the Sufi mystics put it beautifully, there is only one thin veil remaining between us and the Lord. We can already make out the outlines of our real nature—abiding joy, unshakable security, and infinite love. But we do not reach this state overnight. We must have been repeating the mantram as often and as sincerely as we can for many years; and for the vast majority of us, we must have been practicing meditation sincerely and systematically also. Even then, the mystics of all religions tell us, we cannot become completely established in the mantram except through what I can only call divine grace. We must put in the effort; otherwise the Lord will not take us seriously.

But in the end it is only he—or she, as Sri Ramakrishna would say of the Divine Mother—who will open the doors of the Holy Name and take us in.

When this happens, there is a marvelous sense of security that comes, for you know that the mantram can never let you down. It has taken root deep in your consciousness, and as soon as a negative emotion begins to arise, the mantram automatically transforms it into tremendous positive power. For my mechanically minded friends, I sometimes say this is like having a transformer inside with a thermostat attached. When a negative emotion like fear or anger begins to rise, the thermostat sends the message, "Things are getting a little hot down here," and the mantram transformer switches on. Most of us become aware of these negative emotions only after they have risen to the surface level of consciousness, when they have gathered tremendous momentum. But the mantram transformer intercepts fear and anger and greed while they are still in the formative stages, deep in the unconscious, and converts them immediately into immense constructive power. This is why Saint Bernard of Clairvaux calls the mantram "the energizing Word."

When you have managed to become established in the mantram like this, there are really no negative emotions left; every little cranny of consciousness has been flooded with light. There are no selfish desires anywhere, hiding in the basement or in the back of a little cubbyhole of the mind; there are only selfless desires for the welfare of all. It is not that you have no feelings at this stage: if I may say so, it is only at this stage that you really know what sensitivity is, because you are so close to the unity of life that you feel the joy and suffering of everyone around you as your own. The difference is that now, grief or sorrow at the suffering of others opens the door to deeper resources for alleviating that suffering, and will not let you rest until you have done everything you can. To take only one very small example, I feel terribly grieved when I see millions of people, particularly young people, taking to smoking under the influence of massive advertising campaigns, in spite of the overwhelming evidence we have today of the damage smoking does to the body. But instead of going in for diatribes against the tobacco industry, I take every possible opportunity to help people give up smoking through the repetition of the mantram and the practice of meditation.

All spiritual disciplines converge by the time we reach this state, just as all the great religions converge for the man or woman who has realized the Lord in his or her own consciousness. At this stage—but only at this stage—there is very little difference between repetition of the mantram and meditation and total concentration on something outside, because our consciousness is unified from the surface to the very depths. Then concentration is our natural state, and it becomes effortless and natural to focus our complete attention on anything we are doing. When we are talking to someone, we see no one but him, hear no one but her; and when we give our complete attention like this, people cannot help but respond. We can turn our attention to any problem and penetrate to the heart of it, which is the secret of genius in any field. Now, however, we will see only the unity of life, and all our energy will be directed to solving the biggest problems we face today—violence, the despoliation of the environment, the disintegration of the family.

Sri Ramakrishna tells us that being established in the mantram is like receiving a pension after many years of faithful service. When a professor retires as professor emeritus, his pay is sent regularly to his home. He still has a little pigeon hole on the campus where his mail comes, but he doesn't have to do any work if he doesn't want to, like grading examinations or sitting on committees. In my university days in India, I knew many of these professors emeritus who were more regular than many of the regular professors. When you are a regular professor, you sometimes feel a little reluctant to go to the campus or sit down to work, because you know that you have got to do it. But when you become professor emeritus there is no one to compel you to work, so you are free to work just for the joy of it. You come in regularly, you get your pay, you have your privileges and your honors, but you don't have any responsibilities. Similarly, when you become established in the mantram, the Lord, whose employees we all are, says, "You have been working all these years, repeating the mantram and observing the other disciplines from nine to five and on nights and weekends too. You can sit back now, and I will repeat the mantram for you." Of course, like the professor emeritus, you can still repeat the mantram consciously if you like; the Lord will not dock your pay. Shankara, a great mystic of medieval India, says that when you repeat the mantram consciously like this after becoming established in it, when you have nothing further to gain for yourself, the mantram is credited to those to whom you want the credit to go. You repeat your mantram, and those around you who are doing their best to lead the spiritual life will find themselves a little more selfless, a little more secure.

Of course, these marvelous developments do not take place overnight. The mantram begins its work of purifying our consciousness long before we reach the unitive state. At first, most of the work goes into trying to open the door of our mind a little so that the mantram can slip in. Once it gets in under the surface level, it

Nilgiri Press
Box 477
Petaluma
California
94952

stamp

Nilgiri Press publishes books on how to lead the spiritual life in the home and the community. Ask your bookstore about them—or complete this card and mail it to us and we will send you a catalog of our other books.

Thank you.

Name ....
      Please print or type.

Street ....

City ....

State .... *Zip* ....

Date ....

can go on with its work of purification even when we are not consciously repeating it. But at first, it is all we can do to open the door of the mind even a little crack. All the time that we are repeating the mantram at the post office, while walking, while washing dishes, while falling asleep, we are working away at opening that door to our consciousness. When we can use the mantram to overcome likes and dislikes or to change old habits, we are beginning to open the door just a little, and when we learn to repeat the mantram to transform fear and anger and greed, we are not only opening the door but turning on the porch light and putting out the welcome mat, too.

Once the mantram gets its foot in the door, it looks around inside and sees what a messy housekeeper the ego is. The ego doesn't dust, it doesn't sweep, and it can't stand to throw anything out, so our conscious-ness is bulging with photo albums, old projects we lost interest in halfway through, tapes of agitated conver-sations with our friends twelve years ago, even old childhood toys. The mantram slips inside and begins to straighten up the living room; it clears out the cob-webs, throws out the old magazines, and opens up all the windows to let in a little fresh air. Compared to this, those stables Hercules had to clean were like the house beautiful, but gradually the mantram will go through everything room by room. Only when the entire house is spotless from cellar to attic is it ready for its rightful owner: the Lord.

Even in the early days, there are several sure signs that the mantram has begun its work of purification. One sign is that you will hear the mantram occasionally in your sleep, either in a dream or in the state of dreamless sleep. In a dream, the mantram can save you from all sorts of unpleasant situations. Perhaps you have always been afraid of Dracula and sometimes dream that he is pursuing you. You try to run but your legs get heavier and heavier, as if you were wading through quicksand. The panic mounts. Just then you hear the mantram and Dracula disappears, along with all sense of fear. The mantram has come to your rescue, and not just to save you from one unpleasant incident; it is quite likely that this particular fear has disappeared from your consciousness permanently.

Sometimes, too, you may hear the mantram echoing deep in your consciousness, not necessarily in connection with any dream. It will have an unearthly beauty and clarity which will haunt you when you wake up. During the following day you will not be able to recapture just how it sounded in all its beauty, but the mere memory of it will fill you with joy and security. This will give you added incentive to try harder in all your spiritual disciplines, because you know that sustained effort is what really enables you to drive the mantram deep into your consciousness. But there is a danger here of dwelling on such experiences and getting elated over them. For a long, long time they will be like angels' visits, few and far between. So let me suggest that you regard experiences like these not as experiences to be sought in themselves, but only as a sign that the mantram is gradually sinking into your consciousness. Even if you never hear the mantram in your sleep, as long as you are looking for opportunities during the day to repeat it, especially in training the senses and putting others first, you can be sure that it is taking root.

When you hear the mantram in your sleep, you are not consciously repeating it; this is the mantram at work on a deeper level of consciousness. To become established in the mantram, you must be able to repeat it consciously far below the surface level of thought and action. For this to take place, I cannot stress too much how important it is to make use of every opportunity during the day and night to repeat the mantram. Even then, it is not just the number of times you have said the mantram which takes you to a deeper level but the sincerity and enthusiasm with which you say it, as well, combined with the other spiritual disciplines like meditation. I have no hesitation in saying that you cannot become established in the mantram unless you have also reduced your self-will to a very considerable extent. These two go together. Self-will is devotion to "I," which the mantram transforms into devotion to the Lord.

When we have unified our consciousness through these powerful disciplines, not only do meditation and the mantram come together, but all mantrams come together too. Whether our mantram is *Rama, Rama* or *Jesus, Jesus* or *Hail Mary* or *Om mani padme hum,* it fills us with the same joy and security, and it reverberates in the depths of our consciousness with the same beauty. There is a beautiful hymn in Sanskrit called *The Thousand Names of the Lord,* meant to inspire us with a thousand divine attributes of the supreme Reality we call God. Many of these names are used as mantrams in the Hindu tradition, but great mystics like Gandhi have proved in their life that all these thousand Holy Names are contained in the single name *Rama,* as mentioned in the scriptures. This is to tell us that once the mantram has become an integral part of our consciousness, all mantrams are the same. Whatever Holy Name we use, at this stage it is the perfect embodiment of the Lord of Love.

The Holy Name reverberating in the depths of consciousness transfigures our entire vision of life. Just as the mantram transforms negative forces in consciousness into constructive power, so it now transforms all our perceptions of the everyday world into unbroken awareness of the unity of life. When I go for a walk on the beach my ear hears the waves crashing and booming against the shore, but my mind hears them as *Rama, Rama, Rama*. This is not something I try to do; it's simply how I hear it now. And when I hear the birds singing, their song too becomes *Rama, Rama, Rama*— with different accents, with different harmonies, but the final perception is the Holy Name. It is the same with the breeze, with music, with everything. As Swami Ramdas says, the name *is* God, not a symbol but reality; and when we are established in the mantram, established in awareness of the Lord, everything for us is full of Rama—full of joy.

Suggestions for Further Reading ✿

There is a great deal of literature on mysticism and the spiritual life, but by and large it is best to go straight to the writings of the mystics themselves. This list selects a few books that are positive, practical, and inspiring; it is not meant to be comprehensive. Except when noted otherwise, the editions cited are currently available paperbacks; in many cases, other editions are available also.

ANTHOLOGIES OF MYSTICAL LITERATURE. For a general introduction, there are some useful collections which draw on the traditions of all the great religions: *The Perennial Philosophy,* by Aldous Huxley (Harper & Row, 1970); *The Portable World Bible,* ed. Robert Ballou (Viking, 1944); and *Mysticism,* by Frank C. Happold (Penguin, 1963).

CHRISTIAN MYSTICISM. Some of the classics in this rich tradition are *The Confessions* of St. Augustine (many editions; the translation by F.J. Sheed [Sheed & Ward, 1942] is particularly reliable); the *Little Flowers of St. Francis* (Doubleday, Image, 1958); *Meister Eckhart: A Modern Translation,* ed. Raymond B. Blakney (Harper & Row, 1941); *The Autobiography of St. Teresa of Avila,* tr. E. Allison Peers (Doubleday, Image, 1960); *The Imitation of Christ,* by Thomas a Kempis, ed. H.C. Gardiner (Doubleday, Image, 1955); *The Story of a Soul: An Autobiography,* by St. Theresa of Lisieux, tr. John Beevers (Doubleday, Image, 1957); *The Practice of the Presence of God,* by Brother Lawrence (Spire, 1958); and *The*

Way of a Pilgrim, tr. R. M. French (Ballantine, 1974). Evelyn Underhill's *Mysticism* (Dutton, 1961) is a thorough study of Christian mysticism.

HINDU MYSTICISM. The most practical work in Hindu mysticism is the Bhagavad Gita. My own translation and commentary, *The Bhagavad Gita for Daily Living* (3 vols.; Nilgiri Press, 1975–   ), draws out the practical applications of this timeless scripture. A very readable translation, without commentary, is *Song of God: Bhagavad Gita,* tr. Swami Prabhavananda and Christopher Isherwood (New American Library, 1944). *Ramakrishna and his Disciples,* by Christopher Isherwood (Simon & Schuster, 1959), *Ramana Maharshi and the Path of Self-Knowledge,* by Arthur Osborne (Weiser, 1954) and *Gandhi the Man,* by Eknath Easwaran (Glide, 1973; Nilgiri Press, 1977) are good introductions to three of India's greatest modern mystics. An excellent study of Hindu mysticism is Swami Prabhavananda's *Spiritual Heritage of India* (Doubleday, Anchor, 1964).

BUDDHIST MYSTICISM. The Dhammapada is probably the distilled essence of many of the Buddha's sermons. There is a good translation in *The Teachings of the Compassionate Buddha,* ed. E. A. Burtt (New American Library, 1955). *The Gospel of Buddha,* ed. Paul Carus (Open Court, 1973), and *Footprints of Gautama the Buddha,* by Marie Byles (Theosophical Publishing House, 1967), are intimate accounts of the Buddha's life and teachings.

JEWISH MYSTICISM. Martin Buber's *Tales of the Hasidim* (2 vols.; Schocken, 1947) is a good introduction to one of the most appealing expressions of Jewish mysticism.

ISLAMIC MYSTICISM. Good introductions to the Sufi tradition of Islamic mysticism are *The Conference of the Birds,* by Farid ud-Din Attar (Weiser, 1969) and *Rumi: Poet and Mystic,* tr. R. A. Nicholson (hardcover; Allen and Unwin, 1950).

Index ❧

Library of Congress Cataloging in Publication Data:
Easwaran, Eknath.
    The mantram handbook.

    Bibliography: p.
    Includes index.
    1. Mantras. 2. Spiritual life. I. Title.
BL624 . E17   294 . 3'4'43   77-3222
ISBN 0-915132-10-9

ON THE COVER is a selection of mantrams from the world's religions. Here they are identified, transliterated, and translated, from top to bottom and left to right.

Latin: *Ave Maria gratia plena, dominus tecum; benedicta tu in mulieribus, et benedictus fructus ventris tui.*
Hail, Mary, full of grace, the Lord is with thee; blessed art thou among women, and blessed is the fruit of thy womb Jesus.

Arabic: *Bismillāh ir-Rahmān ir-Rahīm.*
In the name of Allah, most gracious, most merciful.

Greek: *Kyrie ēmon Iesu Christe Ie Theou eleēson ēmas.*
Our Lord, Jesus Christ, son of God, have mercy on us.

Chinese: *Na-mo A-mi t'o-fo;* Japanese: *Namo Amida butsu.*
I bow to the Buddha of infinite light.

Hebrew: *Barukh attah Adonai.* Blessed art thou, O Lord.

Russian: *Gospodi isusye khristye, suynye bozhiy, pomiluye mya greshnogo.* Lord Jesus Christ, son of God, have mercy on me, a sinner.

Sanskrit: *Haré Rāma Haré Rāma, Rāma Rāma Haré Haré, Haré Krishna Haré Krishna, Krishna Krishna Haré Haré.*